PRACTICAL
Reconciliation

Strengthening Relationships for
All Australians in 7 Easy Steps

**MUNYA ANDREWS
CARLA ROGERS**

First published by Ultimate World Publishing 2020
Copyright © 2020 Munya Andrews & Carla Rogers

ISBN

Paperback - 978-1-922372-66-6
Ebook - 978-1-922372-67-3

Munya Andrews & Carla Rogers have asserted their right under the Copyright, Designs and Patents Act 1988 to be identified as the authors of this work. The information in this book is based on the author's experiences and opinions. The publisher specifically disclaims responsibility for any adverse consequences, which may result from use of the information contained herein. Permission to use information has been sought by the authors. Any breaches will be rectified in further editions of the book.

All rights reserved. No part of this publication may be reproduced, stored in or introduced into a retrieval system, or transmitted in any form, or by any means (electronic, mechanical, photocopying, recording or otherwise) without the prior written permission of the authors. Any person who does any unauthorised act in relation to this publication may be liable to criminal prosecution and civil claims for damages. Enquiries should be made through the publisher.

Cover design: Ultimate World Publishing
Layout and typesetting: Ultimate World Publishing
Editor: Hayley Ward
Illustrator: Rhys Paddick

WARNING: Aboriginal and Torres Strait Islander viewers are warned that this book may contain images and voices of deceased persons.

Ultimate World Publishing
Diamond Creek,
Victoria Australia 3089
www.writeabook.com.au

Testimonials

An essential primer on reconciliation and a practical guide for a kinder, more tolerant Australia. The authors understand that while Australians share this aspiration, the enemy of action is not knowing where to start and not believing we can make a difference. The book provides a practical road map to the small steps we can all take, and in the process is revelatory and empowering. The writing is conversational, authentic and wise.

It is a valuable reference, an eminently useful book that you will return to again and again. It unpacks the big issues and is embedded in universal values, providing a framework for deeper learning. It draws us in close with information about Aboriginal culture, language and spirituality, instilling a sense of awe and shared pride in who we are as a nation. It is hard-hitting on the importance of listening and bearing witness. This book more than delivers as an action plan, it opens our hearts and minds.
– **The Honourable Justice Helen Wood**
Supreme Court of Tasmania

This is a very practical book and a great starting place to help people understand the issues involved in conciliation between Aboriginal and Torres Strait Islander and non-Aboriginal Australians. If you don't know about our history (like the war for possession of the Australian soil over the last 230 years), it is very hard to have a decent conversation. And this is what this book is about; decency and practical conciliation.
– **Bruce Pascoe, Author,** *Dark Emu*

What an insightful and accessible book full of suggestions for a person and organisation to be more culturally aware and respectful. I strongly recommend this book to all and especially to organisations committed to reconciliation.

— **David Liddiard, OAM**

As people learn more about this country's devastating history, how this land was stolen and that it was never ceded by First Nation Peoples, they know we have to acknowledge and address our unfinished business if we are to become a truly reconciled nation. However, many feel daunted about how to begin to engage. Munya and Carla offer a much-needed practical guide for people to personally or collectively take action. This is a timely and important book.

— **Senator Rachel Siewert**

There have been some welcome additions in recent decades of books about our Indigenous cultures. Now, Munya Andrews and Carla Rogers have made a valuable contribution to that literature. They are skilled and experienced in helping people to better understand Aboriginal cultures. They have combined that experience in this readable and informative book. Not only that. They have done so in ways that are practical and actionable. If this is an interest of yours, this is a book for you to read.

— **Bob Dick, Author,**
Approaching Change, One Story at a Time

Dedication

For all Australians. Together we'll create a kinder Bandaiyan (Australia).

Contents

Testimonials	iii
Dedication	v
Foreword	ix
Preface	xi
Introduction: What is Practical Reconciliation?	xiii
Chapter 1: Reconciliation is for Everyone	1
Chapter 2: Our Mob – Who We Are	15
Chapter 3: White Australia has a Black History	37
Chapter 4: Communication – Unpacking Your Cultural Baggage	57
Chapter 5: Kinship – They're All Related!	79
Chapter 6: Closing the Privilege Gap	103
Chapter 7: Becoming an Ally	115
Chapter 8: Engagement and Cultural Protocols	123
Next Steps – What you can do	145
Glossary	147
Bibliography	153
Stay Connected	155
Special Offer	157
Speaker Bio	159

Foreword

The disparities of our present are intrinsically linked through intergenerational trauma to the pain and injustices of our past.

Australia cannot separate itself from its history. Reconciliation is everyone's business, and we all have roles to play.

It cannot be left solely to First Australians to champion or advocate. And we must always remember that meaningful and lasting change means bringing people with you.

When we look back at the history of this nation, and the statistics which illustrate the division between Indigenous and non-Indigenous Australians, Reconciliation can seem an overwhelming concept.

I can understand how individuals throw their hands up in the air and feel it is beyond them to play any meaningful role.

By breaking down Reconciliation into simple, reasonable and practical steps, the authors enable individuals to take ownership of their contribution to Reconciliation in this country.

They help us understand the need for Reconciliation and the link between the pain of the past and the problems of the present.

And this is essential – as Reconciliation is a journey. Its success is contingent on all the people we bring with us along the way. This book is an important contribution to that journey.

The Hon Linda Burney, MP

Preface

Just over 3% of our population in Australia is Indigenous. So that means that about 1 in every 30 people is Aboriginal or Torres Strait Islander. Imagine we are in a classroom of 30 children. For reconciliation to happen, that one Indigenous person should be sharing the effort equally with 29 other people. Unfortunately, in practice, it's the one out of the 30 that carries most of the burden and impact.

Let's start preventing this by not leaving the burden of responsibility on the few. We have no choice about where or to whom we are born, but we can choose to learn the history of our country. We also have a great opportunity to open our eyes to history's impact on our First Nation's people and our relationships with one another. This book is intended to be part of that learning.

We invite you to read this book and then do something. Take action. No matter how small. Don't leave it to that one person—we can all do something to create a kinder and more inclusive Australia.

Consider this book as a stand-alone companion to our training series and our Seven Steps to Practical Reconciliation™ approach. Although our training takes a deeper dive into the core competencies within each of the seven steps, this book is an excellent primer for those who want to know the mechanics of how practical reconciliation can become a reality for their organisation.

The chapters of this book run congruently with our training program and seven step approach. Each chapter builds upon the previous one, so we recommend that you read the chapters in consecutive order. At the end of each chapter, we've placed a recap of the most important points for your review. We also include a link to an online interactive resource for you to go deeper.

Before we delve into the main content of this book, in the introduction we'd like to share with you our individual and joint journey towards reconciliation and what led to this publication. Much of the book is written from both of our perspectives. For first-person accounts, you'll find our name under the section title. We've also provided a glossary at the end that we hope you will find useful.

Inyjidigal Gorna (Go Well in Bardi),

Munya and Carla

Introduction:
What is Practical Reconciliation?

> *At its heart, reconciliation is about strengthening relationships between Aboriginal and Torres Strait Islander peoples and non-Indigenous peoples, for the benefit of all Australians.* [1]
>
> **Reconciliation Australia**

Practical reconciliation is the actions you can take to make a difference towards creating an inclusive and honest national identity and strengthen relationships. It begins with a desire to connect, and when this desire is combined with proper training and strategy, real connections are forged.

Having trained tens of thousands of people to connect with, acknowledge and celebrate the original inhabitants of our beautiful country, we believe that practical reconciliation is a burning desire of many, if not most, Australians.

---

[1] Reconciliation Australia website. See https://www.reconciliation.org.au/what-is-reconciliation/

Unfortunately, many people just don't know how or where to start. Some people might be frightened of doing or saying the wrong thing, and unintentionally offending. Others might feel paralysed by guilt or shame.

In this book, we include ideas about the things you can do and more importantly, the things to know to make practical reconciliation an integral part of your cultural awareness journey. Like our training programs, the book is a journey of self-reflection, taking you through seven core cultural competencies - the seven steps. We see each step as the most important things that we need to know, understand, be or do for practical reconciliation, focused on:

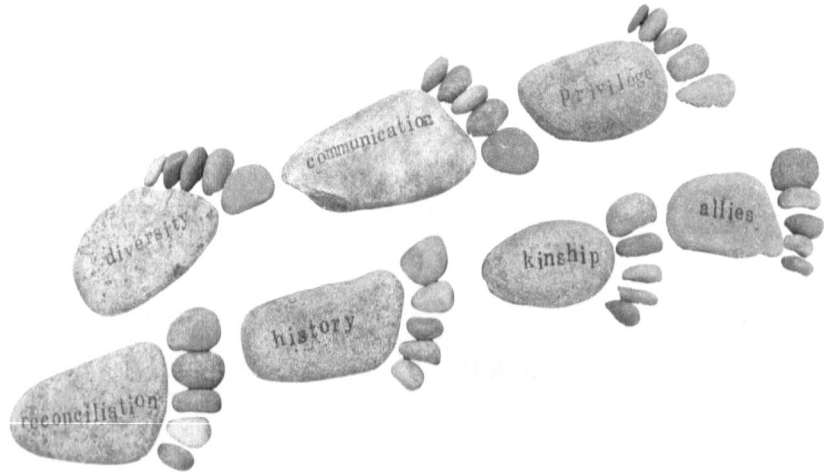

The Seven Steps to Practical Reconciliation™

1 - Reconciliation - an Approach

2 - Diversity, Identity, and Stereotypes

3 - Our Shared History and the Stolen Generation

4 - Communication and Cultural Baggage

Introduction: What is Practical Reconciliation?

5 – Kinship and Sorry Business

6 – Closing the Gap and Privilege

7 – Becoming an Ally

BONUS CHAPTER – Engagement and Cultural Protocols

Taking Action

The common denominator in practical reconciliation is the willingness of individuals to take the first step toward change. From there, it's simply the desire to continue putting one foot in front of the other until the gap that divides us closes. This is not unlike what we experienced as two individuals from different environments. We both realised early on that our similarities with other groups and cultures outweigh our differences. At this point, we share a brief history of our personal reconciliation stories and how they've impacted the work that we do today.

Munya's Story

As a little girl growing up in the small, remote town of Derby in Western Australia, I'd look out at the mudflats at the back of my school and wonder what lay beyond. This natural curiosity led me to learn more about the world I lived in, my Aboriginal culture, and the culture of others. I grew up in a period of Australia's history that was rife with prejudice, discrimination and segregation. I was born at the Derby *Native* Hospital in 1960. During that time, official government policy dictated an apartheid-like policy of treating Aboriginal and non-Aboriginal people in separate medical facilities.

I remember how poorly Aboriginal people were treated by gudia (non-Indigenous people) and the hardships they endured. This was also a sad time when many Aboriginal children were forcibly removed from their families, a practice known as the Stolen Generations. The policy of removing mixed-race Aboriginal children from their mothers was allegedly because of the belief that Aboriginal peoples were dying off. Others see it as a deliberate act of genocide.

Although Aboriginal people and their cultures were not held in high regard by gudia, I refused to believe the lies and negative stereotypes about my people. My deep-seated desire to live life beyond the societal constraints of the time led me to not only fully embrace my heritage but to also create a path of connection with other people from a broad range of cultures and backgrounds. I am fully committed to the reconciliation process and see it as an important undertaking to contribute to a kinder, more inclusive Australia.

Carla's Story

I was born at Sutherland Hospital in Sydney. I have two older brothers and grew up in the Illawarra, NSW. My heritage is a fairly common mix of England, Ireland, Scotland and Wales, with eight convicts, one of those being on the first fleet. From a young age, I had an acute sense of our Aboriginal ancestors and spirits of the 'old people'. I don't know where this came from, but I would wander through Sydney's bush and talk to them - feeling their presence and at times seeing them. Even so, I did not know a living Aboriginal person and hungered for a connection or friendship. I felt an acute emptiness and longing.

You can imagine my excitement when in Year 4, we were told that we would be learning and performing a song about Aboriginal children.

Introduction: What is Practical Reconciliation?

Bingo – combining my love of singing with my thirst for knowledge and connection. There I was, 9-year-old me, singing my heart out on the steps in front of a church in the late 70s.

The song? "Five Little Piccaninnies". Piccaninny is a word applied originally by people of the West Indies to their babies and more widely referring to small children. [2] While in some areas it is not derogative, in others it is, especially in North America where this song was written. I can still smell the old-school-style 'photocopy' of the song lyrics with pictures of curly-headed, dark-skinned babies. When I asked what the song was about, I was incorrectly told, Aboriginal babies. This is perhaps my first vivid memory of *terra nullius* in my schooling. Not only were we misappropriating someone else's culture, but it was as if Aboriginal children did not exist. Unfortunately, however, it was a common thread that weaved throughout my education and early career.

When I left school, I made a beeline to the Kimberley and Kakadu when my friends were mostly travelling to Europe. It is coincidental that years later I met Munya who is from the Kimberley.

I started my career as a cadet town planner. My last job in government was jointly managing the Aboriginal heritage section for the NSW National Parks and Wildlife Service. My longing for an Aboriginal friend motivated my life journey toward Reconciliation. I recall being afraid that when given the opportunity, I would say the wrong thing or second-guess myself. I have made mistakes, but I've learnt many things by sharing my vulnerability with others who in turn directed their kindness toward me. They say that you teach what you most need to know. I guess it makes sense that I now work with an amazing team that has the opportunity to teach the principles of practical reconciliation.

---

[2] https://en.wikipedia.org/wiki/Pickaninny

Evolve's Story
Carla

In 2001, with the help of a Churchill Fellowship, I travelled overseas to explore better ways to engage with communities, with a focus on how Indigenous people were involved in protected area management (e.g. National Parks). After the experience, I returned full of excitement, brimming with ideas. I knew I wanted a platform to share what I'd learned with more people, so I founded Evolve Communities in 2005.

Fast forward six years, and we were leading a project with two remote Aboriginal communities in North Queensland. Evolve's team of facilitators were coaching and mentoring the community to tackle some very hard issues and conversations while developing community safety plans. At the last moment, one of the leading team members had to pull out, and through a high recommendation, Munya stepped in.

To our delight, Munya and I discovered that we had the same core desire and values. That desire was to create a kinder, inclusive Australia that celebrates and recognises our First Nations people. That every person – no matter their heritage – has wisdom to share and values in common. Those values are to connect, create and contribute. In 2014, Munya joined Evolve as co-owner and Director, and together we've created a comprehensive cultural awareness learning framework and program. Since our inception, tens of thousands of people and hundreds of organisations have participated in our programs.

Note: A word on the use of the term 'reconciliation'.

To reconcile means to restore friendship and resolve differences. Many people rightly argue that given our history of invasion and that friendship and respect was never established or offered to Aboriginal and Torres Strait Islander peoples, there's nothing to reconcile.

Introduction: What is Practical Reconciliation?

In this context, 'conciliation', which means to become friendly or agreeable, is more apt.

However, the intent of the reconciliation movement in Australia, and of organisations like Reconciliation Australia - is about strengthening relationships between Aboriginal and Torres Strait Islander peoples and non-Indigenous peoples, for the benefit of all Australians.

Most people come to us and our cultural awareness training with a genuine intent and desire to have meaningful relationships with Aboriginal and Torres Strait Islander peoples and to do something to overcome inequality between Aboriginal and non-Aboriginal people.

The 'term' Reconciliation is a positive action that opens the door to a meaningful and deep learning experience. Therefore, we have used the term in this book.

Takeaways

- Practical reconciliation is the actions you can take to make a difference towards creating an inclusive national identity and strengthen relationships.

- The common denominator in practical reconciliation is the willingness of individuals to take the first step toward change.

- Some people think that the policy of removing mixed-race Aboriginal children from their mothers (Stolen Generation) was because of the alleged belief that Aboriginal peoples were dying off. Others see it as a deliberate act of genocide.

- In practical reconciliation, mistakes will be made. Learning from those mistakes and sharing your vulnerability goes a long way toward compassion and acceptance from others.

> ### **Action:**
>
> This book is designed to be interactive. For this reason, you'll find signposts along the way that will lead you to a special resources section of our Practical Reconciliation website.
>
> These resources are exclusively available to readers of this book and are designed to go hand in hand with it.
>
> Access these resources at practicalreconciliation.com

CHAPTER 1

Reconciliation is for Everyone

Step 1 - Reconciliation

A Practical Approach – R3 Culture®

As the first step, we're excited to share with you our R3 Culture® model. It is an approach to collaboration and reconciliation that can be used in your personal life, work and business and that can help you with all communications and relationships, especially in becoming an ally (more on this in chapter 7).

It may be surprising to hear that a simple three-step approach can make a profound impact on something as layered as cultural collaboration, but it's true. Everything that we share is from personal experience, so you can trust us when we say that it works, even when in a situation where you just want the floor to open and gobble you up.

But before we have a look at where, how and why you would use it, let's have a quick look at what this system includes.

Reflect Relate Reconcile®

Whenever a situation arises that raises a question, confusion or conflict, you can:

Reflect: Pause. Identify the issue
Relate: Try to imagine how the other person might be feeling
Reconcile: Design a way forward together

How it Came About

We have spent many years in the trenches learning from the 'School of hard knocks', especially when we acquired projects that no one else seemed to want. We found ourselves pulling from our previous career experiences in the areas of 'peacemaking' and mediation to find creative solutions that worked.

When conflict arises within a large group (as it often will), there are a number of things that we found useful to do. Our approach to transforming conflict involved nine steps. But really, in the heat of the moment, who is going to remember nine steps!

As we have matured, we have tried to make things simpler and more memorable. We pooled our experiences and condensed the nine steps into three, known as the R3 Culture® approach.

Evolve's R3 Culture® Approach

How does it work? In our cultural awareness workshops, we have people practice the approach with real-life scenarios. Below we share some stories from our 'real life' experiences:

How we Dealt with our Grief for Truganini with the 3Rs

Munya and Carla

Truganini, Wikimedia Commons

It is one thing to have heard of someone, quite another to be standing in their country and land of birth, reading their life story.

The sun bounced off the ocean on a crisp autumn day as we stood on what is known as 'the neck,' a narrow strip of land connecting north and south Lunnawannalonna (Bruny Island), Tasmania. We were at the fifth timber stair, to climb another 235 that led to spectacular views along with a monument in honour of Truganini and the Nuenonne people, the original inhabitants of Lunnawannalonna.

We stopped to read a sign about Truganini, one of the most familiar names in the story of Australian colonisation. Many Australians know of Truganini. Often described as the 'last' Tasmanian Aboriginal, a historic claim that is deeply misleading and untrue. We read the sign in front of us that shared a few hard-hitting facts about Truganini's life - a small part of her story which is as tragic as it is heart and gut-wrenching.

> *As a child Truganini grew up here at Lunnawannalonna. Her father was an Elder of the Nuenonne people, a band of the south-east tribe whose connection with this place spanned some 30,000 years. The peace of Truganini's early years was shattered by European invasion. The arrival of the white man brought violence and brutality to these shores. At the age of 17 Truganini witnessed the horrific stabbing of her mother by men from a whaling ship. Sealers kidnapped her two sisters, Lowhe-nunne and Magger-leede. Timber-getters killed the man Truganini was to marry. During a boat crossing of the channel, she watched in horror as her husband to be was thrown into the sea. As he tried desperately to climb back onboard the timber-getters cut off his hands and left him to drown. Truganini was then repeatedly raped. Her brother was killed, and her stepmother kidnapped by escaped convicts. Her father was devastated and died within months.*

The immediacy of this tragedy juxtaposed against eager visitors racing past us to get that perfect selfie was surreal, to say the least.

We did notice however an older international tourist from Singapore taking the time to also stop and read the sign fully before tackling the remaining stairs.

Our guided tour then took us to Adventure Bay which was the departure point for the Bruny Island Wilderness Cruise: "Cruise alongside some of Australia's highest sea cliffs, beneath towering crags and drift up close to listen to the awesome 'Breathing Rock'. Enter deep sea caves, pass through the narrow gap between the coast and 'The Monument' and feel the power of nature at the point where the Tasman Sea meets the might of the Southern Ocean."

Overall it was an outstanding experience, but we found it unsettling that the introduction given by the engaging and passionate guide lacked an acknowledgement of the original custodians of Lunnawannalonna. Historical references were made to the 'explorers', with Adventure Bay being named after Captain Tobias Furneaux's ship 'The Adventure' in 1773. We were told about the area being visited by Furneaux and also Captains Cook, Bligh, D'Entrecasteaux and Tobin in the 1700s, but that was it.

We waited for the guide to continue with acknowledgement of the Nuenonne people and especially of Truganini given her significance in Australia's history, which sadly, did not come.

We were distressed when the talk progressed to the whaling industry, and then just moved on. The trip and the staff's professionalism were outstanding in every other aspect; however, a big part of both of our thoughts remained with Truganini. It felt like (yet another) annihilation of truth and obliteration of this land's original custodians.

So how did we move through this?

Let's take another look at the 3Rs:

Reflect – Stop. Pause. Consider what led to this situation

Relate – Put yourself in the other person's shoes

Reconcile – Find a solution, where possible, with that person

Considering our options, one would be to approach the guide, but before taking action, we decided to walk through the 3Rs:

Reflect: We returned to our hotel and researched Bruny Island and the Nuenonne people. We discovered that tourism was a relatively new and growing industry. We also found that land had been handed back to Aboriginal people on the island – a working farm known as Murrayfield Station which contains significant Aboriginal sites.

Relate: The passion, commitment and desire of the guides to do the right thing and look after passengers was evident. It was a professional outfit. With a different perspective, they might be willing also to acknowledge the Nuenonne people and especially Truganini.

Reconcile: We wrote to the cruise operator to share with them our experience and ask what 'Acknowledgement of Country' is normally given. Perhaps its absence was irregular. We suggested that an appropriate acknowledgement be given and offered assistance to support this.

It reinforced for us the importance of acknowledging Country whenever and wherever we travel in Australia, whether it be in the bush or the city, and that this is the heart of the 3Rs – to reflect, relate and reconcile, and have an open heart and mind to mutual learning.

Note: There are several other spellings of *Truganini's name, including Trugernanner, Trugernena, Trugannini, Trucanini, Trucaminni,* and *Trucaninny. Truganini* was also widely known as *Lalla(h) Rookh.* [3]

---

[3] See the Wikipedia article, "Truganini".

Practical Reconciliation

Climbing Pigeon House (My Father's 80th Birthday)

Carla

Jim Rogers on his 80th birthday mountain climb

My father, Jim Rogers, is an adventurous soul who decided that for his 80th he would climb the 720 metre Pigeon House mountain, within Morton National Park, on the South Coast region of New South Wales, Australia. NSW National Parks warns that: "The hike is pretty intense (Grade 4), with steep inclines and ladders to reach the summit, the perfect hike for people with a good fitness level and a sense of adventure."

So, our excited party of 15 set out to the summit where my father would proudly pose for the epic group photo. It was a public holiday with plenty of other hikers, but none of those sporting a T-Shirt declaring their qualification as an Octogenarian. My daughter, Talise (who was 10 at the time) and I started a bit behind due to a last-minute pit stop.

Not wanting to miss out on the summit photo, I was anxious to catch up with the rest of the group. However, it quickly became evident that Talise was not a happy hiker. She was limping and becoming increasingly frustrated at the nagging mother (me) urging her to walk faster.

She finally stopped in frustration and tears, and I thought to myself, "Okay, time to stop and practice what I preach".

So, we sat on a rock. Clearly, it was time for me to apply the 3Rs.

Reflect - Only the week before I'd taken Talise to a physiotherapist about a sore ankle and foot. She was obviously in pain and not enjoying herself. I was the one getting carried away with my ambition to get to the top.

Relate - While on that rock, I asked myself how I would feel in Talise's shoes. My passion for bushwalking came later in life, and when I was 10, the last thing I'd want to do is hike up a steep hill, especially with a sore ankle and a parent nagging me to go faster.

Reconcile - I asked Talise what we could do to make this a more pleasant experience for both of us. She replied: "Well mum, how about I lead, we walk at my pace and stop when we need to? If we get to the top, great but if not, well does that really matter?" Yes, wisdom from the mouth of a tween.

The result? It was a pleasant stroll rather than a race to the top! But in slowing down into the grace and ease of a walking meditation, my thoughts slowed, allowing me space to observe. It occurred to me that while charging up that mountain, I didn't do any of the things that I've been taught. Didthul Mountain is sacred to Aboriginal People. Did I really think that they would have raced to the summit as though it were a marathon? I noticed that I hadn't acknowledged Country. So, we picked up some stones and threw them ahead of us on the track "Hello old people, it's Carla and Talise, thank you for letting us visit your sacred mountain today. We are here to celebrate my father's 80th, we hope it is okay". We then waited until it felt okay to move forward.

And you know what? We eventually made it to the summit. My father was still there. We had an incredible walk that brought us closer to each other and the mountain itself.

They're Always Late for Work

This story was told to us by one of our training participants, Paul, and it is a brilliant workplace example. Kane was a new Aboriginal trainee who had moved from Western Australia to Canberra to work in the public service. Kane was consistently late for work, and other team members were starting to complain behind Kane's back about what they felt was a 'slack' attitude. Paul, although not directly working with Kane, was concerned about him and how he might be finding it difficult to settle in. So, Paul applied the 3Rs:

Reflect - Kane was new to the city and possibly had no family or friends. Some members of the team felt Kane's lateness was an issue but did not seem to be addressing it with him or his supervisor.

Relate - Paul imagined how scary it would feel to move from a country town to a city where you had no family or friends. Paul invited Kane to have a coffee, to chat about how he was finding the move.

Reconcile - In the conversation, Paul learned that Kane did not have a car and did not know how to get the right pass to catch the bus, or even how to catch a bus. There was no public transport where Kane grew up. This was why he was frequently late. Otherwise he really enjoyed the job. So, they agreed that Paul would get a bus pass with Kane and they'd catch the bus to and from work until Kane was comfortable to travel alone.

This is a great example of not only applying the 3Rs but of practical reconciliation.

Why Can't I Give a Welcome to Country?

Munya

During one of our cultural awareness workshops, a non-Indigenous man asked me, "Why can't I give a Welcome to Country? I'm an Australian, and I would like to welcome people to this land too." I had never been asked that before, so I used our R3 model to help me answer it.

Reflect - This young man has a different understanding of what a Welcome to Country means and what it's all about.

Relate - Our philosophy at Evolve is that there is no such thing as a silly question because we want participants to feel safe. Therefore, I need to be open-minded and patient to respond to his question.

Reconcile - I acknowledged his intention to welcome people to Australia before explaining that we are talking about a traditional Indigenous custom and how to do it properly. The first protocol is that we never speak on behalf of the rightful traditional owners. So, while he can welcome people to the land, he just can't do it on behalf of the local cultural group.

But What If?

We hope that through these stories you can find examples of how you might be able to Reflect, Relate and Reconcile.

But you still may have some doubts.

For example, how can you put yourself in another person's shoes? What if you get it wrong?

Well, that's a great point. At Evolve we teach people about unconscious bias and assumptions (see Step 4.) In doing this, we urge people to become aware of their assumptions and biases and when they might be acting on a belief that is not true. So, are these things mutually exclusive? Is it possible to empathise without making assumptions? Yes and No.

You have to make some guesses and assumptions when relating to someone. However – and this is key – the most important thing you can do is listen with an open heart and mind. Ask yourself if you have made any assumptions. You can then share these with the other person.

In the example of Kane, the first assumption that you might check out is, if in fact he has been late. So, after checking in with Kane about how he is, you could say something like "I have noticed once or twice that you have arrived at work a bit later than the start time, but I could be wrong about this. How do you see it?"

In terms of relating, you could say something like: "I have been imagining how I might feel having moved away from family to a new job and big city. I think I'd feel scared and not sure how things work. But this may not be how it is for you at all. I'd really love to hear more about how it is for you".

Chapter 1 Takeaways

- The R3 Culture approach stands for Reflect, Relate, and Reconcile.

- It is an approach to collaboration and reconciliation that can be used in your personal life, work and business that can help you with all communications and relationships.

- Reflect – Pause and identify the issue. Relate: Try to imagine how the other person might be feeling. Reconcile: Design a way forward together.

- Conflict does happen and, in many cases, if handled well, conflict can be transformative. Embrace compassionate curiosity when conflict arises.

- Acknowledging Country whenever and wherever we travel in Australia is an essential component of practical reconciliation.

- We invite you to think about a situation where you can apply the 3Rs – even at home, have a go and please share your experience with us.

Action:

Download your copy of the R3 Culture® guide at practicalreconciliation.com

CHAPTER 2

Our Mob - Who We Are
Step 2 - Diversity

Practical Reconciliation

A great starting point to explore cultural diversity among Indigenous people is the Indigenous Map of Australia designed by David Horton and published by the Australian Institute of Aboriginal and Torres Strait Islander Studies (AIATSIS) in Canberra. Often referred to as the 'languages' map, it depicts a colourful mosaic of the various Indigenous nations of about 250 or so. When we show it to people and ask for their first impressions, reactions include: "Incredible, colourful, diverse".

Indigenous Map of Australia, David Horton, AIATSIS ©

The sheer number of Indigenous tribes or nations is eye-opening for those Australians who have never considered the diverse number of groups that make up the country. Comparisons are often made with Europe albeit on a much grander scale. It tests assumptions and stereotypes of Indigenous people and makes participants realise that when it comes to developing policies and programs for Indigenous people, with all this cultural diversity, clearly, one size doesn't fit all.

In our cultural awareness training, we encourage participants to find out as much as they can about the different nations, especially the nation in which they live or work. Also, to learn how to pronounce their correct names as a mark of respect. For instance, many people often get the Aboriginal nations Wiradjuri and Wurundjeri mixed up. Wiradjuri is the largest Aboriginal nation in New South Wales, whereas Wurundjeri is the largest in Victoria. The difference is not just a matter of semantics but cultural as well.

We encourage organisations to display the map in their workplaces to help Indigenous staff and clients feel culturally safe. It also serves as a valuable cultural resource and tool for all Australians to learn more about Indigenous people and their history before the arrival of their European forebears. It's also a wonderful opportunity for Indigenous people to find out more about their cultural history. For example, during one of our training workshops in Hobart, Tasmania, a fair-skinned Aboriginal man identified himself to Munya as a Bundjalung man from Stradbroke Island in Queensland. He was somewhat perplexed as to why his family identified as Bundjalung because Bundjalung country is in northern New South Wales near Byron Bay. Munya shared with him a story that she had been told by a Bundjalung Elder in Lismore.

According to Aunty Lorraine Mafi-Williams and stories told by her people, Stradbroke Island once straddled the coast off Byron Bay long ago before travelling northward to its current position off the Queensland coast. The travelling island carried with it its Bundjalung occupants, which is why they still identify as Bundjalung and speak the language. This cultural information made complete sense to the man who previously was at a loss to explain his Bundjalung heritage.

The moral of the story is that some amazing cultural knowledge and insight can arise out of exploring the map, asking questions and having conversations. Who knows what you might discover!

While there is disagreement about the veracity of some tribal boundaries, the map is an ongoing collaboration between the designer and Indigenous nations. AIATSIS are quick to point out that the map is not definitive, but for the most part it is generally accepted as a good depiction of what exists and is relied on by many different groups and organisations.

Although we designed our cultural awareness training as an introduction to Indigenous issues, we impress upon participants the importance of building partnerships of trust with their local communities. This allows them to continue their cultural education to make them aware of this diversity of opinions and proposed solutions.

Indigenous Diversity

Australia's Indigenous Peoples and Indigeneity

When it comes to practical reconciliation, we need to be clear about who is Indigenous and who is not. In terms of practicality and administration, the Australian government officially recognises two separate groups as the Indigenous peoples of Australia. Essentially, these are the people who were here long before the arrival of Europeans and their colonisation of Australia. They include the Aboriginal people of the Australian mainland and offshore islands, and Torres Strait Islanders who are Indigenous to the Torres Strait region of northern Australia. Despite similarities, these two groups have significant linguistic and cultural differences between them that are considered below.

Indigeneity is a new-fangled word. Like Aboriginality, it refers to the quality of being Indigenous or Aboriginal. It's comforting to hear others using the word, such as Aboriginal actor, Uncle Jack Charles, who describes himself as a 'leading black light'. A special bond exists between all Indigenous peoples from around the world. Whether this is because of our shared life experiences of colonisation or similarities in philosophical approaches to life is not clear, but the connection they feel is palpable. Or as a well-known t-shirt says, 'It's a black thang'.

Who is Indigenous?

Practical Reconciliation

The question of who is Indigenous is a vexed issue in Australia where Indigenous people are confronted and challenged to explain their need to express a separate cultural identity from other Australians. Government has struggled with this issue through the years – there being something in the vein of 66 definitions or so. The latest definition is three-pronged. To be officially recognised as Indigenous, you must:

1. Be of Aboriginal or Torres Strait Islander descent
2. Identify as Aboriginal or Torres Strait Islander person, and
3. Be recognised as such by their community

Of course, this is the government definition, not necessarily a view shared by Aboriginal or Torres Strait Islander peoples. For some, it is simply enough to come down the line. In other words, biological descent is paramount. Nor does it matter how far back you can trace your cultural heritage, whether it is 3, 5 or 500 generations. Given that Aboriginal people are intermarrying, the gene pool is quite colourful these days. It's not uncommon for Indigenous people with fair skin and blue eyes to identify as Indigenous. For Indigenous peoples, it's all about biological descent and socialisation, i.e. whether you are brought up as Aboriginal or Torres Strait Islander. This is something mainstream Australians struggle to grapple with but there is a popular saying among Indigenous people who jokingly remark, "A cup of tea is still a cup of tea no matter how much milk is added!"

Aboriginalitea

Respectful Terminology - Colonial Versus Indigenous Names

When dealing and communicating with Indigenous people, it's important to get the terminology right. The first thing to realise is that terms like Australia, Aboriginal, Indigenous and Torres Strait Islander are colonial not Indigenous. In other words, they are names that have been given by the colonisers and are not names that Indigenous people have traditionally used to refer to themselves.

Generally, Indigenous people prefer to use their own names like Bardi or Bundjalung, or to speak their own language. But they accept that Australia is now an English-speaking country and will use these terms albeit somewhat reluctantly or with constraint.

We're often asked in our training if it's okay to refer to Indigenous people as Aborigines, for example. Our response is, well if you do, technically you're correct because it comes from Latin, meaning original people. But as we point out, Aborigine is an old-fashioned term and rarely used. If they must go with a colonial term, most prefer the adjectival Aboriginal. Then again, some people regard Indigenous as an umbrella term that mixes the two groups together – Aboriginal and Torres Strait without recognising the two groups as being culturally distinct. This speaks to some of the underlying political tensions that exist between the two groups.

At Evolve, we use both terms interchangeably and always endeavour to work with the different groups as to what terms are suitable for *them*. The term Indigenous came into vogue as an all-encompassing term for native peoples around the world and through the application of International Law in our domestic laws. In much the same way, First Nations people has entered the Australian lexicon and is used in a similar fashion.

Torres Strait Islanders

Torres Strait Islander is another imposed term. The Torres Strait is named after the Spaniard explorer, Luis Vaez de Torres, who passed through the Strait in 1606. Of course, it was unknown by that name to the people who lived there who have their own names for the region and the individual islands that make up the group. Even though the Torres Strait region occupies a smaller geographic area than continental Australia, it is just as culturally and linguistically diverse as Aboriginal Australia.

The islands fall into four regional areas comprising the Northern, Eastern, Central and Western Islands with two communities located on the Australian mainland, Bamaga and Seisia on the tip of the Cape York peninsula. The main languages spoken are Meriam Mer, Kala Lagaw Ya and Torres Strait Kriol. Ever since the publication of Bruce Pascoe's ground-breaking, seminal book *Dark Emu*, people are less inclined to characterise Torres Strait Islanders as an agricultural society versus the 'nomadic' Aboriginal people as a point of cultural distinction.

Through extensive historical and other research, Pascoe has questioned and overturned previous claims of Aboriginal people as being nomadic with no tradition of agriculture or settled communities. Granted, there are significant cultural differences between the two groups but not along the lines of one being more 'civilised' than the other.

There is a sizeable, growing population who identify as Aboriginal *and* Torres Strait Islander, thereby forging closer ties and bonds than ever before. This is not to deny there are some political tensions between the two groups of people as to which group is Indigenous to Australia. One way of avoiding this is to point out that Torres Strait Islander people are Indigenous to the Torres Strait whereas Aboriginal people are Indigenous to the Australian mainland and offshore islands such as Tasmania, Kangaroo, Stradbroke and Tiwi Islands to name a few.

Early in the 20th Century, the Torres Strait came under the jurisdiction of the Australian government through state legislation under various Queensland Acts. Like Aboriginal people, Torres Strait Islanders were subject to restrictive legislation and government policies that denied them many civil rights, including loss of sovereignty over their islands.

As a matter of convenience, the Australian government lumped them under the Indigenous umbrella and proceeded to treat both groups as though they were one homogenous entity. Of course, nothing can be further from the truth and Torres Strait Islander people have asserted their rights to be treated as a separate cultural entity with their own flag and Native Title rights. We mustn't forget either that although they were the first peoples to be granted Native Title in Australia they were not the first who fought for Native Title. The Bardi and Jawi peoples of the Kimberley were put forward as a test case alongside Eddie Mabo, the former being the more successful of the two.

Australia or Bandaiyan?

Even the name Australia is a colonial term. Possibly because it was not taught at schools, many Australians don't know where the term comes from or what it means. It comes from Latin for *Terra Australis Incognito* or Unknown Southern Land. [4] Most people get the *Terra Australis* part but often leave out the 'Unknown'. They also often mistake it for 'Great Southern Land' as in the pop song by Australian rock band, Icehouse. We say to people, it's important to refer to the whole phrase *Terra Australia Incognito* because of its implications for Australia being declared *Terra Nullius* – Empty Land or 'Land belonging to no one' by the invaders. Matthew Flinders popularised the term Australia by placing its name on maps drawn by him. [5]

Of course, Australia was not unknown, unloved or unnamed by its Indigenous people. In the Kimberley where Munya comes from, this land is known as Bandaiyan. Bandaiyan incorporates the Gaia concept that the land is a breathing, living, sacred, sentient being. Bandaiyan is a bisexual being lying on their back in the Southern Indian and Pacific oceans. Its head is in the north, its lungs extend across the Pilbara, Northern Territory and Queensland. Uluru is not the heart of Australia as the tourist industry would have you believe but is instead the navel or sacred omphalos. The southern states represent the genital region and Tasmania is not forgotten as its legs extend out under the Southern Ocean where its left foot pops up. [6]

Within the body of Bandaiyan lies the Rainbow Snake, the supreme creator. Right across Australia, Aboriginal people have stories about the Rainbow Snake who is said to have created our world. As Worrora

---

[4] See Wikipedia article "Terra Australis".
[5] See Wikipedia article "Australia".
[6] David Mowarljarlai & Jutta Malnic, *Yorro Yorro*, pp. 190-191.

Elder, David Mowaljarlai from the Kimberley writes in *Yorro Yorro*, "She grows all of nature outside of her body." [7]

What's interesting about this Aboriginal model of Australia is that it demonstrates that Indigenous people were aware of the length and breadth of this country. It also reveals how Aboriginal people as far away as the Kimberley knew of the existence of Tasmania through their songlines and trading routes.

What's Wrong with Indigenising the Country?

There are many place names in Australia that retain their Indigenous names but there is also much confusion. One can only wonder why renaming some towns or landmarks such as Uluru for Ayers Rock and Gariwerd for the Grampians in Victoria causes outrage to some Australians. How can using Indigenous names or speaking an Indigenous language be so threatening? We can all take pride in our Indigenous heritage whether you are Indigenous or not. It is a treasure for all to share.

Indigenous place names are important not just for preserving cultural heritage but for the ecological and environmental information they contain. These place names describe the availability of certain plants or environmental information relating to water supply and seasonal factors impacting on food and water availability. They may also refer to poisonous foods and sickness country that warn people of the perils that surround them. So, it's not just about pandering to the whims of Indigenous people or being politically correct. Sometimes it's about our survival in this nation and learning more about the world in which we live.

---

[7] Ibid, p. 191.

Generic Versus Traditional Names

In addition to their own Indigenous names for themselves, some generic or pan-Aboriginal names are used. These terms are not necessarily tribal but came about because of colonisation during a time when Aboriginal people were removed from their families and lost knowledge of their tribal affiliations. Feeling alienated in white Australian society and being treated very differently to other Australians meant they needed to assert a separate cultural identity that was Indigenous based rather than European. Generic terms such as Koori, Murri and Nunga filled the void by becoming catch-all phrases for those having identity issues.

Pan Aboriginal Names in Australia

Naming the Other

Just as white Australians imposed their collective names on Indigenous people, so too they developed names for the invaders. However, unlike some disparaging names of Europeans for Aboriginal and Torres Strait Islander people, Indigenous names for the newcomers like balanda, gubba, gudia, migaloo and wajella are non-derogatory. Often, they describe skin colour like gudia and migaloo or are a corruption of an existing word such as balanda for Hollander to describe the Dutch in northern Australia or wajella and its variants such as walbala for whitefella. Gubba comes from governor or government representing the state, which interacted with Indigenous peoples from the beginning.

'Same Same', 'Same Kind' and 'Same Kind But Different' - Homogeneity Versus Heterogeneity Indigenous Style

When making comparisons between different cultures, it's useful to think of what we have in common, i.e. how homogenous we are and the things that make us different from one another, i.e. heterogeneous. Indigenous peoples express these concepts in Aboriginal English as 'Same Same' or 'Same Kind'. So, as Munya explains, when people ask how she relates to Bundjalung people (east coast) as a Bardi woman (west coast), she will say, "We same same or same kind" meaning she shares similarities by being Aboriginal. But when she wants to emphasise the cultural differences between Bardi and Bundjalung, she will say, "We same kind but different."

This applies between gudia and Indigenous peoples as it does between the different Indigenous nations. Another way to think of this is as differences within and without. So, within Australia there are cultural differences that exist between the nations and without Australia explains the cultural differences that exist between Aboriginal and Torres Strait Islander people or between Aboriginal people and other cultures such as gudia and other newcomers to the land.

The Aboriginal and Torres Strait Islander flags

These differences are expressed in ways one would expect such as through art, dance, dress, food, languages (kriols), music and even colours. We observe the latter in the different colours of the Aboriginal and Torres Strait Islander flags and their cultural associations. On the Aboriginal flag for instance, red stands for the land on which we live, black for the Aboriginal people and yellow for Mother Sun, the giver of life. By contrast, the colours of the Torres Strait Islander flag have green for the land, blue for the waters surrounding the isles, black for the people and a white headdress called dhari. All cultures associate colours with different things and have different meanings. Aboriginal and Torres Strait Islander people are no exception. Red is a very sacred colour to Aboriginal people as it not only represents blood, the vital signs of life, but red ochre that has strong cultural meanings and significance.

In considering what Aboriginal and Torres Strait Islander people have in common, three things stand out: Indigeneity, Spirituality and our Connection to Country or the land.

Spirituality

Closely aligned to Indigeneity is Spirituality. Many Indigenous cultures around the world are characterised by an all-embracing, all-encompassing spirituality that is Earth-centred, guided by spirit ancestors and shamanic practices. Aboriginal people refer to their spiritual traditions as Dreamtime or Dreaming. Once again, the Indigenous names vary across the country such as Tjurrkupa, Lalai or Nyitting. Although Torres Strait society is highly Christianised today, their traditional spirituality is akin to Aboriginal Dreamtime. In fact, one Torres Strait Islander man told Munya they are one and the same. However that may be, many Indigenous people draw on their spiritual traditions to guide them through life and many derive their group and personal identity from their beliefs. This not only includes traditional spiritual beliefs but also other religions.

It's important to know about Indigenous spirituality for lots of reasons but especially how it might impact on Aboriginal and Torres Strait Islander peoples' work performance and career pathways. It may help to explain unaccounted absences from work because of spiritual obligations to look after Country or for spiritual mischief, where people account for their aberrant behaviours due to other people 'singing' them for instance. Rather than dismiss these cultural explanations as irrational or superstitious, a more empowering and respectful approach is to work within that cultural framework. If you are a manager of Indigenous staff experiencing these issues, it is best to work with an Elder or Elders, preferably with someone experienced in this area.

Connection to Country

'Country' is the Aboriginal English expression for land. In its deeper application, it stands for one's tribal lands that gives Indigenous people a strong sense of belonging through their group and personal identity. Indigenous people may refer to their country by specific name such as Bardi or Noongar country or by the land's characteristics. For example, those who live on the coast will refer to their country as 'saltwater country', those who live by lakes or rivers will call their lands 'freshwater country' and those in the desert will refer lovingly to their 'desert country'.

Freshwater, desert and saltwater country

Country is intrinsic to cultural identity. Without Country, there is no self or soul. People's Dreamings and stories are tied to Country, and Country plays a significant role in one's spirituality. With Dreamings come responsibilities for looking after and caring for Country. This includes such things as burning and singing the Country to ensure its fruitfulness and balance. Country must be ecologically maintained to ensure survival of humans, animals and plant life. Country is not seen as something outside of Indigenous existence but rather the most important reason or purpose for someone or something's existence, what the French describe as raison d'être. In some Aboriginal cultures, Country is regarded as family. And just like family, people feel sorry for Country, cry for Country and sing for Country. During the 2020 Australian bushfires where people experienced devastation on an unprecedented grand scale, the loss of Country was mourned by Aboriginal people who cried for the damage done to Country and to our animal and plant brothers and sisters.

The connection between land and health is paramount. Land or Country gives Indigenous people a strong sense of well-being. So much so that when the land is damaged and polluted, Indigenous people are damaged and polluted. It gives a very different cultural viewpoint of illness. In fact, Indigenous people have a saying 'Healthy Country, Healthy People' that embodies this holistic philosophy. Whenever Evolve are working with medical or health practitioners, we stress the importance of this nexus and of developing health programs that connect people with Country.

Cultural Protocols

There are many cultural protocols as one would expect of any cultural group, and we go deeper into these in Chapter 8. They involve rules for all manner of things from caring for Country, raising children, maintaining culture and keeping the laws.

The two most important cultural protocols regarding land is the Welcome to Country and Acknowledgement of Country. While most are aware of the difference, sometimes they get them mixed up. A traditional owner of Country where a meeting is held gives a Welcome to Country. An Elder or their representative usually does this. It may include a smoking ceremony but not always. An Acknowledgement of Country, on the other hand, can be given by anyone regardless of whether they are Indigenous or not.

There are many scripted versions and questions about who to include in the acknowledgement. It has become trendy for instance, to include 'emerging' leaders. Our view is that it is enough to acknowledge the traditional owners, without necessarily designating certain groups within that such as children or young people. Care should be taken to identify the *right* people for Country. Indigenous people are like other human beings and there will sometimes be disagreements about tribal boundaries and who are the traditional owners of Country. If you are unsure, seek advice from your local Indigenous land council or a reputable local Indigenous organisation such as the Aboriginal Medical Service or other such body.

Most importantly, learn how to pronounce the traditional name correctly. As mentioned earlier, note the subtle distinctions between some nations such as Wiradjuri and Wurundjeri, for example. It's just common courtesy to not get someone's name wrong and cause embarrassment or offence. For example, pronouncing the name Munya with a British accent, would be telling her to go forth and multiply! So, do take care and if unsure of the correct pronunciation, seek advice beforehand.

At Evolve, we love sharing with our participants our credit-card sized 'Acknowledgement of Country' cards. With these, you always have the right words for this important cultural protocol at your fingertips.

Evolve's 'Acknowledgement of Country' card

Breaking Stereotypes

In our cultural awareness training, we touch upon many stereotypes of Indigenous people, positive and negative. We allow Room for people to raise issues and for healthy and safe discussion to explore these.

Cultural safety is an important principle that guides our training. We are all cultural beings and come from a wide variety of cultures. Personal safety is coupled with cultural safety and we ensure both for our participants. People are encouraged to speak freely from their personal and political viewpoints. Our approach emphasises 'No Blame, No Shame'. We cannot change the past and the terrible things that have happened to Indigenous people. We seek to impart understanding of how certain historic events and government policies have impacted the lives of Indigenous people. We do this to comprehend the whys and come up with culturally appropriate solutions to help alleviate the pervasive problems Indigenous people have faced. A strong emphasis is placed on practical reconciliation and what you can do to make a difference.

Lateral Violence

The issue of Indigenous identity or Indigeneity is often raised when we are exploring and challenging stereotypes of Aboriginal people. It is a vexed issue as it has an enormous negative impact on an individual whose identity is questioned or under attack. Lateral violence is a pernicious practise that describes a form of bullying that is carried out by other members of an oppressed group. Sometimes described as 'black on black violence', it differs from other types of bullying where the violence is directed top/down where power dynamics are far more obvious as opposed to horizontal violence where bully and victim are on equal footing. While we don't go into lateral violence as part of our general cultural awareness training, we do address the issue in specialised workshops designed specifically for managers of Indigenous staff.

Lateral violence may account for Indigenous staff leaving their workplaces because the issue has not been dealt with properly by people unaware of its existence and lacking in appropriate skills to deal with the issue. Thus, it is a hidden problem in Indigenous staff retention.

Chapter 2 Takeaways

- For many Australians, the 250 diverse groups that make up Indigenous tribes or nations in Australia is eye-opening.

- Indigeneity and aboriginality both refer to the quality of being Indigenous or Aboriginal.

- When dealing and communicating with Indigenous people, it's important to get the terminology right. The first thing to realise is that terms like Australia, Aboriginal, Indigenous and Torres Strait Islander are colonial not Indigenous.

- Australia is a colonial term that comes from Latin for *Terra Australis Incognito* or Unknown Southern Land.

- Indigenous place names are important not just for preserving cultural heritage but for the ecological and environmental information they contain.

- 'Country' is the Aboriginal English expression for land. In its deeper application, it stands for one's tribal lands that gives Indigenous people a strong sense of belonging through their group and personal identity.

Action:

How much do you know about Aboriginal and Torres Strait Islander peoples? Take the quiz at practicalreconciliation.com

CHAPTER 3

White Australia has a Black History

Step 3 - History

We bet that caught your attention! This was the NAIDOC theme for 1987. It was considered a controversial slogan at the time primarily because we had not advanced far in our reconciliation journey to understand that this slogan can be read in two ways – positive or negative.

The negative aspect of a 'black history' speaks to the terrible atrocities that happened to Aboriginal people since colonisation – the murders, the massacres, the slavery and imprisonment – often for offences they didn't know they'd committed – and the dispossession of Aboriginal and Torres Strait Islander people.

They're not easy things to talk about, but the fact is, they happened, and they had a devastating impact. But it doesn't mean we can't or shouldn't talk about those things. People say, "Oh why can't they just get over it and move on."

So, why can't they just get over it and move on?

At a recent conference a participant, Jan, confided:

"I've been dying to ask this but didn't know who to ask and I really don't want to offend anyone. My 14-year-old daughter came home from school the other day upset about having to do 'this silly acknowledgement of Aboriginal people at the beginning of assembly'. I actually agree with her. I don't understand why they do this and why people just don't get over it and move on".

In the brief time we'd been with Jan, we'd experienced her as a kind and generous person. This was a question coming from genuine curiosity, not malintent. We often get this question asked in our workshops, and fortunately we have at least half a day for people to reflect and find an answer within themselves.

In this instance, we had only a few minutes. So, we answered from a deep knowing:

"Jan, there's nothing to move on from. How can you move on from something that you are experiencing now"?

Carla then went on to share Amy's story:

"Only yesterday I met Amy, a resilient, inspiring Aboriginal woman. Amy was tired and I asked her why. She explained that she'd been up late the night before ironing her children's school clothes, so they were immaculately presented. I was gobsmacked. I make a point of buying clothes that don't need ironing. As far as my daughter goes, I have never thought twice about sending her off in a crumpled uniform. I was horrified that because of the colour of her skin, Amy was judged more harshly than me based on ironing. This is also a great example of my privilege as a white person. I don't have to think about the consequences of a simple thing such as not ironing.

However, when I asked Amy about it, her response was next level. She was from the Stolen Generation and was removed from her family at a young age, growing up in an institutional home with "little love, support or guidance". She then revealed to me that one of her deepest fears is having her own children taken from her, so she irons her children's clothes to ensure that they leave the house immaculately dressed.

This, along with many other things, is happening today.

It's not about 'just getting over it and moving on'. It's about acknowledging what happened and understanding that there are consequences of human actions that leave a trail of trauma that has long-term effects. In any community, a difficult or traumatic time for a person can affect their children and their grandchildren in negative ways. This is called *transgenerational trauma* and is prevalent in Aboriginal and Torres Strait Islander communities. This is due to the generations of people who have been affected by many traumatic events.

The Oldest Surviving Culture

The positive aspect of the slogan 'White Australia has a black history' reminds people that Australia wasn't uninhabited, that there were black people living here before white people. It is all about celebrating with pride the achievements and history of Indigenous people in this land we now call Australia.

Did you know that in Australia, we have one of the richest and oldest continuing cultures in the world? That is an incredible and powerful realisation. Just think about that for a moment. What does the word 'surviving' mean to you? To us, it means that Aboriginal culture is not something that existed only before 1770. It goes a long, long, long way back to over 100,000 years and is still thriving today. Think about that for a moment. The next time you walk down the street you are likely to pass someone whose ancestry goes back tens of thousands of years.

Carla was incredibly privileged to work with the Aboriginal descendants of Mungo Man and Mungo lady - the Paakantji, Ngyiampaa and Mutthi Mutthi people, in Western NSW. "Mungo Lady and Mungo Man are perhaps the most important human remains ever found in Australia. Their discovery re-wrote the ancient story of this land and its people and sent shock-waves around the world". [8]

Mungo Man and Mungo Lady (as they are popularly called) lived around the shores of Lake Mungo with their families around 42,000

---

[8] See http://www.visitmungo.com.au/mungo-lady-mungo-man

years ago. They are the oldest remains of modern humans (Homo sapiens) yet found outside of Africa. Mungo Lady is the oldest known cremation in the world, [9] and Mungo Man the oldest known ritual burial:

"His family mourned for him, and carefully buried him in the lunette, on his back with his hands crossed in his lap and sprinkled with red ochre. Mungo Man is the oldest known example in the world of such a ritual." [10]

If you haven't been to Lake Mungo in Western New South Wales, we urge you to get there at least once in your lifetime. Mungo lady was the daughter, and Mungo man the son, of many mothers, the generations before them that lived at Mungo since the Dreamtime. And today we consider it a gift to walk, live and learn alongside their descendants.

What has our History got to do with it?

On one level, it's simple. If you want to follow the basic tenet of treating others how you would have them treat you, you show kindness and care, whether it be a friend or colleague. You listen. You find out what makes them laugh, what's important to them, what makes them sad.

For practical reconciliation, this is no different. And an important part of that is understanding our shared history and the past events in Australia that are still causing pain. Australia Day is a case in point. It is incomprehensible that we celebrate this day in history as the 'official' national day of Australia.

---

[9] Ibid.

[10] See http://www.visitmungo.com.au/who-was-mungo-man

Australia Day marks the anniversary of the 1788 invasion of the First Fleet of British ships at Port Jackson, New South Wales, and the raising of the flag of Great Britain at Sydney Cove by Governor Arthur Phillip. Compared to 100,000 years of Aboriginal people living, loving and sharing this land with each other, the 230 years since invasion is minuscule. It was less than 100 years ago in 1935 that all Australian states and territories adopted use of the term 'Australia Day' to mark the date, and less than 30 years ago in 1994 that the date was consistently marked by a public holiday on that day by all states and territories.

While happily ensconced in a retreat at Bundanoon one Australia Day, Carla captured her feelings below:

Musings on 'Australia Day' by Carla

They say they are invisible
Just not there
Claims of extinction
"Well, I have never met one, have you?"
Sits uneasy this feeling of unrest
As their spirit eyes settle on me
I shift my gaze to avert

Why do I choose this blindness?
Deaf to their calls
Unfeelingly to their touch
Easy! Denial is easiest
Terra Nullius assuages the guilt
Of the invasive murderer that I am
However unwitting

So what is to celebrate?
Pause.
Much

That they see me
And despite our best efforts
They survive, No thrive....
Like snake tendril roots through rock

Perhaps eventually engulfing, encasing, entombing
This frightened spirit
That dares not look
At the truth....
This Country...
Always was. Will be.
Yours.

So just imagine that tomorrow we are invaded by another country, who raise their flag, take possession of our homes, and throw us into purpose-built jails. If that isn't bad enough, imagine that years later your grandchildren and great-grandchildren are asked to celebrate that day as a national holiday. Unthinkable, really. This would be like an Aboriginal person claiming England for our First Nations people.

Aunty Munya claiming England on behalf of Aboriginal people.

But, this is our reality and we believe this is largely the result of not acknowledging our shared history. According to Reconciliation Australia:

"There is a discernible lack of appreciation by settler Australia about the grievances and sense of historical injustice that Indigenous people feel. This must be addressed for Australia to be reconciled. Bridging that schism is the Reconciliation movement's greatest challenge." [11]

There are so many reasons why understanding our history matters. We must first know where we've been as a nation before we can know where we are going. This means acknowledging our Indigenous people, who were here first, as a mark of respect. This doesn't mean that all other people who came later are unimportant or of no consequence. It's about understanding dispossession and colonisation and how this has impacted race relations in this country. We have observed a real hunger in many people to know more as well as a feeling of being let down by an education system that doesn't always embrace the true history of Australia.

In their 2018 study, Reconciliation Australia [12] found that:

- The majority of non-Indigenous Australians report low to no knowledge of Aboriginal history, except for the Northern Territory, where 73% of respondents cite a high level of knowledge.

- Most non-Indigenous Australians in 2018 believe it is important for all Australians to learn about past issues.

---

[11] Patrick Dodson, Foreword, "The State of Reconciliation in Australia: Our History, Our Story, Our Future", *Reconciliation Australia*, 2018, p. 4.
[12] Ibid.

- Most Australians believe it is important for reconciliation to create a formal process to enable truth-telling about the wrongs of the past.

- The clear majority of non-Indigenous Australians accept that there were more than 250 Indigenous Nations at the time of colonisation.

- Most Indigenous and non-Indigenous Australians support Indigenous histories and cultures being taught in schools.

Reconciliation Australia says we will know we are reconciled as a nation "when, and only when there is widespread acceptance of our nation's history and agreement that the wrongs of the past will never be repeated – i.e. there is truth, justice, healing and historical acceptance." [13]

In a National Press Club address, celebrated Australian author Richard Flanagan examines a divided Australia which he says can only be free if it faces up to its past:

"The prosperity of contemporary Australia was built on the destruction of countless Indigenous lives up to the present day, and with them Dreamings, songlines, languages, alternative ways of comprehending not only our extraordinary country but the very cosmos." [14]

As a nation, if we dared to acknowledge both truths about our past, "we would discover …. the new people who came to Australia, in their dealings with black Australia, were also Indigenised, and, in the mash-up, Indigenous values of land, of country, of time, of family, of space and story, became strong among non-Indigenous

---

[13] Ibid, p. 9.
[14] Richard Flanagan: 'Our politics is a dreadful black comedy' - Press Club speech in full, *The Guardian*, 2020, p. 7. Available online.

Australians. Indigenous ways, forms, and understandings permeated our way of life in everything from Australian rules football to our sense of humour." [15]

Indigenous researchers and authors like Bruce Pascoe are educating other Australians about the benefits of learning from Aboriginal cultural practice and history. His ground-breaking book, *Dark Emu: Black Seeds: Agriculture or Accident?* released in 2014 dared to challenge some of the most deeply-rooted preconceptions of Aboriginal culture held by white Australia. Drawing upon written accounts from gudia explorers such as Charles Sturt and Thomas Mitchell, *Dark Emu* portrays Aboriginal Australia as a thriving and highly competent society, complete with construction, agriculture and engineering.

Our Shared History – the Golden Ribbon Exercise

The term history has evolved from an ancient Greek verb that means "to know, learned, and wise." [16] Aboriginal 'knowing' extends back more than 100,000 years with Dreamtime wisdom. Compare that with Australia's youthful 'shared history' at just over 230 years.

To understand some of this history, we'd like to share with you one of our favourite workshop activities called 'The Golden Ribbon' exercise. The group forms a circle and unravel a golden ribbon, which is a visual image of time. For Aboriginal people, time is circular rather than linear.

The ribbon is 10 metres in length and represents more than 100,000 years of Dreamtime. Toward one end of the ribbon is 1770, when Captain Cook declared Australia as *'terra nullius'* – empty or no-one's land.

---

[15] Ibid, p. 8.

[16] See https://time.com/4824551/history-word-origins/

Imagine standing on that line now and look back towards the Dreamtime. Imagine that your ancestors had loved, cared for and sung the land for this time. Also imagine then that in a matter of moments, your land is declared *'terra nullius'* – unoccupied.

We ask you to take a journey in time with us now. Imagine that you are an Aboriginal or Torres Strait Islander person and it is:

1770 – When Captain Cook enters Botany Bay, you are declared as non-existent by the British Crown – 'terra nullius – land belonging to nobody'.

1788 – The First Fleet arrives and for the first time, you and your family are murdered, incarcerated, forced from your land – and you experience wars, disease, restriction of movement and attempts at forced assimilation.

Throughout the 1800s, you see 3 out of 4 people in your family and community die.

1910 – The Stolen Generations. Although this started with colonisation, government policy now mandates that your children are forcibly removed from your family and raised in white institutions and Aboriginal missions. This practice continued to the 1970's.

1911 – Restrictions mean you are subjected to new laws in all states, giving governments total control over your life, dictating where you can live and be employed.

1928 – For the last time, after many massacres across Australia, the last known officially sanctioned massacre of Indigenous Australians, The Coniston Massacre, occurs in the Northern Territory.

1948 – For the first time you are considered an Australian Citizen, but you still weren't counted as part of the population.

1962 – For the first time you are given the right to vote at Federal elections, but enrolment is not compulsory.

1967 – The Referendum result means that for the first time, you are counted in the national census.

1972 – For the first time, you have some representation in Government with the establishment of the Department of Aboriginal Affairs.

1992 – For the first time, at the Historic Redfern address, you hear a Prime Minister asking non – Indigenous Australians how they would feel if the past injustices inflicted on Indigenous Australians had been inflicted upon them.

Also in 1992 – The Mabo decision, when the High Court of Australia recognises that Native Title did in fact exist and that Australia had not been terra nullius at the time of European settlement.

1997 – For the first time, the extent of the stolen generation and its impact was acknowledged by Government in the Bringing Them Home Report.

2000 – You witness 250,000 Australians walk across Sydney Harbour Bridge to show their support for reconciliation.

2007 – The Northern Territory Intervention. Unfortunately, NOT for the first time, you experience your rights being stripped away, including control on how you spend your money.

2008 – For the first time, you hear a Prime Minister make a formal apology to the Stolen Generations.

2010 – For the first time, an expert panel appointed by the Government develops recommendations to recognise Aboriginal and Torres Strait Islander peoples in our nation's Constitution.

2017 – More than 250 Aboriginal leaders from across the country gather at Uluru and identify amendments required for constitutional recognition of Aboriginal people. However, the government rejects their proposal for a constitutionally enshrined voice to Parliament.

2018 – For the first time, Year 11 HSC students can learn about pre-1788 Aboriginal history in the same way they are taught ancient Greek and Roman history, with a new 'Ancient Australia' unit.

Where does our Shared History fit in?

People are shocked to realise that our shared history of colonisation equates to just over 2cm on the ribbon while other notable world events such as the emergence of Christianity, Buddhism and so-called 'ancient' civilisations (like the ancient Greeks or the ancient Egyptians) occur only within the first three metres of the 10-metre ribbon. When compared to the longevity of Aboriginal culture, these events pale into insignificance. Munya often jokingly remarks, "What's this ancient nonsense? They just youngfellas compared to us!"

Moving further along the ribbon, people soon begin to appreciate that Australia's history extends way back into the past when volcanoes were once active some 9,000–10,000 years ago in Victoria. This expanse of time extends from before Port Phillip Bay became flooded to about 60,000 years ago, when Lake Mungo was a rich wetlands teeming with life. During this time, Aboriginal people lived, hunted and buried their dead in elaborate, funerary rites, involving cremation and the use of ochre.

As participants stand holding the Golden Ribbon, they are asked to imagine these past events, especially that of our shared colonial history. Imagine standing on that line now and looking back towards the Dreamtime. Imagine that your ancestors had loved, cared for and sung the land for this time. Also imagine then that in a matter of moments, your land is declared *terra nullius* (unoccupied).

Participants unravelling the Golden Ribbon

To find out about some of this history we recommend the highly acclaimed historical TV series *First Australians*, which deals with these issues from an Indigenous perspective.

So, what does this all mean?

It means that every Aboriginal person that you meet is still living with the effects of things that happened in the past 230 years.

So far, we've covered just a few key events in history that are important to understand when we talk about reconciliation. In previous chapters, we mentioned the Stolen Generation. We'd like to go a bit deeper in this section so that its relevance and impact today is better understood.

The 'Stolen Generation' are Aboriginal and Torres Strait Islander children stolen from their families and communities through race-based Government policies. Most sources agree that between 10 to 30% of Indigenous people now aged over 45 were removed from their families in childhood (between 1910 and the 1970s). This means tens of thousands of children across Australia. Even today, almost every Aboriginal family has a story to tell about family members who were removed, and this is a very recent history. There are people today as young as their 40s who were stolen.

Transgenerational Trauma

Supporting Aboriginal and Torres Strait Islander people includes listening, bearing witness, and caring about the stories from the Stolen Generation and being mindful of the impact then and now. There are incredible resources out there – books, movies, online interviews, songs and poems where you can gather additional information. Two resources that are a great starting point include the movie *Rabbit-Proof Fence* and Archie Roach's song, *Took the Children Away* which tells his personal story of being taken away from his family.

In these stories, people share experiences of being snatched from their family, of humiliation and prejudice and having their name changed and identity stripped away. Many were told that Aboriginal people were bad, and that their parents and grandparents did not want them. They were denied love, and subjected to physical, emotional, and sexual abuse. They tell of being forced into institutions (homes and being adopted or fostered out to non-Indigenous families). The deep wounds and scars are real and palpable. We see the symptoms today in broken relationships, disconnected families, violence, suicide, and drug and alcohol abuse. The psychological effect of these experiences has been described as transgenerational or intergenerational trauma. This is trauma that is transferred from the first generation of trauma survivors to the second and further generations of offspring of the survivors via complex post-traumatic stress disorder mechanisms. In Australia, transgenerational trauma especially affects the children, grandchildren and future generations of the Stolen Generation. One of the well-known effects of the Stolen Generation is that those having gone through the experience often find it difficult to parent properly because they don't know how to nurture their children because they were denied the opportunity to be nurtured themselves. [17]

To learn more about the impact of transgenerational trauma, we highly recommend the book, *Trauma Trails, Recreating Songlines: The Transgenerational Effects of Trauma in Indigenous Australia* by Judy Atkinson.

Despite this incredible trauma, there is healing that is taking place with the support of ongoing counselling and other services. Increasingly, more Indigenous people are searching for and returning to their families. There are national Aboriginal and Torres Strait Islander organisations like the Healing Foundation (healingfoundation.org.au) who partners with communities to address the ongoing trauma caused by actions like the forced removal of children from their families. There are Link-Up services who help members of the Stolen Generation trace their families and be reunited with them (or their gravesites, country or kin). Archie Roach's powerful song *Took the Children Away* celebrates Aboriginal resilience and the joy of Aboriginal children returning to their families as adults. The 'stolen' children continue to come back today.

---

[17] See https://healingfoundation.org.au/intergenerational-trauma/

Stone Photographs

In our cultural awareness training, Munya shares an emotionally moving story that she was told by a Noongar Elder in Perth in the 1980s. The Elder tells how she found her parents after having been removed as a small child and then returning to the family home years later. The home had changed very little from the time she was removed. She walked into a rudimentary dwelling with none of the modern features one might expect like electricity and running water. There wasn't a wooden or concrete floor but bare earthen ground. When she walked in, she noticed two round rocks covering depressed indents in the ground. She asked the meaning and one parent lifted the rocks to reveal a set of footprints and told her, "This is all we have to remember you by." You see, in those days, very few Noongar people owned cameras, so they had no photographs of their children.

Dog Tags - Exemption Certificates

When doing the Golden Ribbon exercise in our history session, there are many historic events that are unknown to participants, some which are quite shocking. Most people are unaware of Exemption Certificates that Aboriginal people could apply for from 1943-1969. They allowed Aboriginal people to argue that they should no longer be constrained by the provisions of the Aborigines Protection Act and to access social security benefits that other Australians received, including family and old age pensions. Unfortunately, it also meant you had to give up your Aboriginality, to not mix or socialise with other Aboriginal people and not speak your language. What a hefty price to pay in exchange for little or no promised benefits or privileges. It certainly did not improve the overall status of Aboriginal people in Australian society. If anything, it created a separate class of Australians who had to carry their papers always and produce them as required by authorities, including the police. For example, as late as 1959, if you were found on the streets of Perth after 6pm without your papers, you could be arrested and thrown in jail. Little wonder Aboriginal people derogatorily referred to these certificates as *dog tags*.

Doing our Part

So now you know that in Australia we have one of the richest and oldest continuing cultures in the world. What an incredible and powerful realisation. We do indeed have something to feel very proud of and celebrate, all of us, together.

As an ally and for practical reconciliation to occur, you don't need to be a history buff. Practical reconciliation and cultural awareness is not about knowing the facts and figures of history. It's about moving forward together in a shared, proud and strong identity. Moreover, it's helping heal the hurts of the past, listening to people's stories and understanding their pain so that we can become more compassionate, loving beings. We have so much to learn from our Indigenous brothers and sisters.

In the words of Richard Flanagan:

"We are not a new country. We are in the first instance a society that begins in deep time. That is the bedrock of our civilisation as Australians, our birthright, and if we would accept it, rather than spurn it, we might discover so many new possibilities for ourselves as a people." [18]

---

[18] See https://www.theguardian.com/australia-news/2018/apr/18/richard-flanagan-national-press-club-speech-full-politics-black-comedy

Chapter 3 Takeaways

- The slogan 'White Australia has a Black History' can be read two ways – positive and negative.

- Moving on from past traumatic events is not as easy as some people think. Post-traumatic syndrome is a very real psychological condition that takes time to heal from, as is transgenerational trauma.

- Our history is a shared history we all need to come to terms with in a mature and respectful way. We all have our part to play.

- Being an Ally to Aboriginal and Torres Strait Islander people is about moving forward together in a meaningful act of Reconciliation.

Action:

View key events in our shared history, from the perspective of an Aboriginal or Torres Strait Islander person, at practicalreconciliation.com

CHAPTER 4

Communication – Unpacking Your Cultural Baggage

Step 4 – Communication

Critical to any successful relationship is not only communicating effectively with other people but more importantly, being aware of and dealing with your *unconscious bias*. Key to this is understanding what's inside your cultural baggage. Whether we're talking about our unconscious bias or our cultural baggage, they are effectively the same thing – the ways in which we are blinded by our hidden bias and expectations when interacting with others, usually in a cultural setting.

What is Unconscious Bias?

Unconscious bias is learned stereotypes that are automatic, unintentional, deeply ingrained beliefs that affect our behaviour. Thus, most people are unaware of their unconscious bias and their prejudices towards others until they are pointed out (usually by the person negatively affected by these behaviours).

What is Cultural Baggage?

Cultural baggage is a common metaphor to refer to our attitudes, beliefs, expectations, judgements and values. It is the assumptions that you have about yourself, your family, friends and the world based on your own experience. These assumptions (or unconscious bias) influence what we think, say and do, yet we are not even aware of it. As renowned cultural expert, Edward Hall puts it:

"Culture hides much more than it reveals, and strangely enough, what it hides, it hides most effectively from its own participants. Years of study have convinced me that the ultimate purpose of the study of culture is not so much the understanding of foreign cultures as much as the light that study sheds on our own." [19]

---

[19] Edward Hall, "The Power of Hidden Differences," in Milton J. Bennett (ed), *Basic Concepts of Intercultural Communication: Selected Readings*, p. 59.

Why Unpack your Cultural Baggage?

Our cultural baggage is all about our values and ideas of how we *think* people should behave. So, when we come to any interaction, we bring our cultural baggage, filled with our innermost beliefs and thoughts, our personal past and present, our values and beliefs, and a whole bunch of other goodies – even our culture's history and geography.

The question is, how much do we know about what's inside our own bag? Why would you want to unpack it? We suggest it's a way of getting to know ourselves better and learning how to get on better with others, especially those from a different cultural background.

Sprinkled throughout this chapter you'll find examples of Munya and Carla's cultural baggage, and invitations to unpack your own.

Speed Dating with Cultural Baggage Cards

A useful tool for exploring our unconscious bias is unpacking our cultural baggage. This has proved to be one of our most popular and fun workshop activities.

We begin with a speed dating exercise. Armed with a set of Cultural Baggage cards exploring different social behaviours, the facilitator asks participants how they are likely to respond in that situation. An important point to emphasise is that there is no right or wrong answer. There are no shoulds or shouldn'ts, just our first responses and thoughts. The less that we think about what we 'should' say or do, the more honest our response, and the more room for learning and growth.

Are you Ready to Speed Date with us?

If we were in a workshop together now, we'd have the opportunity to hear a range of viewpoints and responses; some like our own and some very different. That is a key lesson in the exercise – to deepen our understanding that behaviours are underpinned by a large array of hidden beliefs, values and assumptions that may differ significantly from other people.

Well, we invite you on a date with us right now. Answer quickly. We know that your response in life would depend on the actual situation. For the purpose of this exercise, don't think about it too much and go with your first reaction.

Are you ready?

Here we go (take a moment to reflect on your response to each question – even better if you can take some notes):

1. When I ask someone a direct question and they don't respond, that makes me feel…

    _____
    _____
    _____

2. When someone doesn't pay attention to me when I am speaking or are silent for long periods of time, that means …

    _____
    _____
    _____

3. When someone lowers their head and doesn't look me in the eye when I am talking to them, that means …

Communication – Unpacking Your Cultural Baggage

_____
_____
_____

4. My first thoughts about someone who is constantly late for meetings and work without a good reason is…

   _____
   _____
   _____

5. The colour black in my culture means….

   _____
   _____
   _____

6. When someone does not say 'please' or 'thank you', in my culture that means…

   _____
   _____
   _____

7. Shaking hands in my culture means….

   _____
   _____
   _____

How did you go? Are you ready for a second speed dating round?

Unpacking your Cultural Baggage

Becoming aware of your cultural baggage will go a long way towards lightening it. For our next date, we share some common responses to the speed dating questions. We then explore key cultural differences or themes to think about when building relationships with Aboriginal and Torres Strait Islander peoples. Remember that, like all people, our First Nations people are as diverse as any other community, so the themes below are generalisations and will differ from community to community and person to person.

When I ask someone a direct question and they don't answer, it makes me feel......

Ignored, sad, sometimes frustrated. Perhaps they didn't hear me. They didn't understand the question. Or perhaps they don't like me or wish to engage. Or they are just not understanding or getting me.

All of the above could be true or not.

Direct questioning is not very common (or polite) in Aboriginal conversation. Direct questions are limited to things like, "Who's your Mob?" and "Where are you from?" In linguistics, these questions are called 'orientation' questions and are usually simple. Aboriginal and Torres Strait Islander people tend to prefer a less direct approach to communication, and direct questioning can be confronting and offensive. The customary way of seeking information is to establish an exchange, volunteering information of their own and hinting at what they would like to find out.

This can be tricky when working within Aboriginal communities where you often need to ask questions. Try asking only one question at a time and don't ask compound questions (e.g. 'Is it this way, that way or the other way?'). Try to avoid questions with double negatives. These occur when two negative words are used in the same sentence. Using two negatives usually turns the thought or sentence into a positive one. Double negatives are generally discouraged in English because they are poor grammar and can be confusing.

Be aware that silence in response to a question may mean that the person does not understand the question, does not know the answer, or may know but is lacking the confidence to reply. They also may know the answer but not be the right person to respond, or they may feel you are not entitled to know the answer because it is a sensitive or taboo topic. You can try asking the question in a different way, and if it was a compound question, break it up. The most important thing is to establish rapport with the other person first, talking about something that might be of interest to the community (for example a sporting or community event). Spend time with that person until they feel comfortable to determine the content, direction and pace of the interaction between themselves and you. This helps build rapport and trust.

When someone doesn't pay attention to me when I am speaking or is silent for long periods of time, my first reaction is that …

They're not interested. They don't care. They are shy and not a big talker. They don't like me. They're bored.

All of the above could be true or not.

When speed dating, we deliberately leave a long pause in the middle of asking this question. Inevitably, someone jumps in to fill that space with something like "sorry, what was the rest of that question?"

How do you react when there are long periods of silence in a conversation?

For many Aboriginal people, silence is as much as part of communication as is talking – it can show respect, contemplation, disagreement, or to allow time to reflect and consider. Sitting in a conversation, you're likely to notice that people are quite happy for long periods of silence, and just to say something every now and again. There is certainly no pressure to keep the conversation going.

When engaging with Aboriginal people, be prepared for long silences and be patient. If you push through your comfort zone and ride the wave of silence, you will find it easier to cope.

We love to play with words here at Evolve and note that an anagram of silent is *listen*.

This speaks volumes!

Dadirri - Deep Listening

No one speaks of the power of deep listening like Aunty Miriam-Rose Ungunmerr-Baumann of the Miriam Rose Foundation. Dadirri (da-did-ee) is from the Ngan'gikurunggurr and Ngen'giwumirri languages of the Aboriginal peoples of the Daly River region in the Northern Territory. Dadirri is inner, deep listening and quiet, still awareness. Dadirri recognises the deep inner spring that is inside us. Says Aunty Miriam:

"We call on it and it calls to us. This is the gift that Australia is thirsting for. It is something like what you call contemplation. When I experience dadirri, I am made whole again. I can sit on the riverbank or walk through the trees; even if someone close to me has passed away, I can find my peace in this silent awareness. There is no need of words. A big part of dadirri is listening. My people are not threatened by silence. They are completely at home in it. They have lived for thousands of years with Nature's quietness." [20]

---

[20] See https://www.miriamrosefoundation.org.au/about-dadirri

We encourage everyone to learn more about Dadirri and Aunty Miriam's work.

When someone doesn't look me in the eye when I am talking to them, that means ...

They're not listening. They're embarrassed, shy, ashamed, or on the autistic spectrum. They might have something to hide or are sneaky. They might be guilty or distrust others.

All the above could be true or not.

In most communities, direct eye contact may be inappropriate and avoiding eye contact can be a sign of respect.

In western cultures avoiding direct eye contact is often perceived as hiding something, being shifty or being dishonest or that the person is not to be trusted. But among Aboriginal and Torres Strait Islander peoples, avoiding direct eye contact is a mark of respect, especially toward Elders or those in authority. So, people will either avert their eyes or hang their heads to show respect.

Gudia people are often said to have 'hard eyes' which speaks to the discomfort a person might feel when staring directly at them. The best strategy is to follow by example and avert or lower one's eyes in conversation. Direct eye contact is especially avoided between the sexes.

Children are taught to hang their heads down and not look Elders in the eye. And yet, what is the first thing that gudia teachers say to Koori kids? "Look me in the eye when I'm speaking to you." What that teacher has done, without realising, is tell those kids to break one of the basic cultural protocols of communication.

As Munya recounts:

"As a child growing up in the 60s, I soon realised that this was something I had to come to terms with, so I would train myself to look gudia people in the eye. I would start slowly for a few seconds, then a minute. Then I would gradually extend my eye contact for longer periods of time to where I am now comfortable with doing this. But other Aboriginal people may not have undergone this training and continue to communicate in an Indigenous way. Now some Aboriginal people may be comfortable with direct eye contact, but most aren't. Remember, we're talking about generalisations."

If an Aboriginal person does not look you in the eye, it can be a sign of respect, and it does not mean that they're not listening

My first thoughts about someone that is constantly late for meetings or work without a good reason is...

They're lazy. Unprofessional. They don't care. They do not respect my time. They think their time is more important. Punctuality clearly does not matter to them. They don't really want to be there.

All the above could be true or not.

Whatever your thoughts on the subject, we need to understand what Edward Hall calls the 'Language of Time'. He says:

"Time is a core system of cultural, social, and personal life. In fact, nothing occurs except in some kind of time frame. A complicating factor in intercultural relations is that each culture has its own time frames in which the patterns are unique. This means that to function effectively abroad it is just as necessary to learn the language of time as it is to learn the spoken language." [21]

Indigenous people joke about it and call it 'Koori time', 'Island Time', 'Fijian time', 'Samoan time' and so on. But the language of time in Aboriginal and Torres Strait Islander cultures is very different from other Australians. This has important implications for building and maintaining partnerships for communities and organisations as it does for the individual. Western cultures place a lot of emphasis on meeting deadlines whereas Indigenous peoples regard relationships as being more important than time. And as sociolinguist Diana Eades points out in *Aboriginal Ways of Using English*, "Aboriginal and Torres Strait Islander people reckon time not by the clock or calendar, but in reference to some social, seasonal or climatic event". [22]

For Aboriginal people, time is all about maintaining relationships, not looking at clocks or watches. Aboriginal and Torres Strait Islander communities are focused on processes rather than outcomes. This

---

[21] Edward Hall, *The Dance of Life*, p. 3.
[22] Diana Eades, *Aboriginal Ways of Using English*, p. 102.

can be the opposite to Gudia culture where outcomes, deadlines and timeliness is important.

What this means practically is that for an Aboriginal person an important cultural responsibility or obligation is more important than turning up on time. If this obligation is more important than a meeting or work, then the chances are that a person might arrive late or not at all.

We are River People, we cannot Hurry the River

Dadirri teaches us patience and stillness of mind. Aboriginal people are extremely patient. They know that within quiet stillness there are answers to life. As Aunty Miriam Rose says:

"Our Aboriginal culture has taught us to be still and to wait. We do not try to hurry things up. We don't like to hurry. There is nothing more important than what we are attending to. There is nothing more urgent that we must hurry away for. We are River people. We cannot hurry the river. We have to move with its current and understand its ways. We hope that the people of Australia will wait. Not so much waiting for us to catch up but waiting with us, as we find our pace in this world." [23]

Sharing my Cultural Baggage

Carla

In my new role as Manager at a local council in regional NSW, I set about finding the Aboriginal Liaison officer and making a meeting with the Local Aboriginal Land Council. The meeting was set for 10am. I was so nervous driving my flash Council car to the Aboriginal

---

[23] See https://www.miriamrosefoundation.org.au/about-dadirri

community (which was previously a Mission). Butterflies going nuts in the tummy, this young white girl do-gooder (not knowing what good I could or would do).

I recall sitting at the meeting watching the time…10:05…10:15. I notice I'm still the only one there. I begin to wonder, are they not going to meet with me? By 10:30, I'm thinking this is ridiculous. I look at my watch. It's now 10:40 and still no one around. I've heard of Aboriginal time but really, this is getting rude now. Finally, at 10:45, an Aboriginal person shows up. That someone was in fact 15 minutes *early* for the meeting.

Daylight savings time had come in on the weekend, and I hadn't changed my watch.

Boom. Sudden realisation.

This was a lightning bolt for me!

Every time I make a cultural blunder like this is when I have assumed something, and then acted on that assumption without checking the facts. In this case, I assumed that I had the right time, and then the assumptions and inferences escalated from there (known as the ladder of inference):

They don't want to meet me

They will think I am a white do-gooder

They are late

They are typically late

They are rude

That was all in a matter of seconds. So, in this instance, people were early or on time.

In my cultural baggage, where we talk about 'deadlines' and 'milestones' and time is considered linear, if you say a meeting will start at 10, then that's when it starts. Starting late or not turning up at all is 'wrong'.

However, within Aboriginal communities, relationships trump time. Time is circular and infinite. There are some exceptions of course. For example, Munya is unfashionably early to meetings. However, if a relative needed help, which made her late for the meeting, her relative is prioritised over being on time as much as she loves to be on time.

More typical of my culture is the famous Good Samaritan study which found that a person in a hurry is less likely to help people. I still find myself falling into the trap of prioritising time and deadlines over relationships. This is part of my cultural baggage. The great news is that the more I unpack my cultural baggage and discover what's inside, the greater understanding, empathy and connection I can have with others.

The colour black in my culture means....

Grieving. Slimming. Death. Funeral. Fashionable. Dark. Depression (e.g. Black Dog) Something bad. Evil. The Bad Guy (e.g. Darth Vader).

All the above could be true or not.

Do you think colours are neutral?

In *The Silent Language,* Edward Hall tells how as a young anthropologist in the 1960s, he went to live and work with the Navajo people in south-western America. At that time, many Navajo were illiterate in English. Tribal council elections were looming and some bright spark in the Indian Bureau (as it was called then) decided to assign different colours to the political candidates to enable them to vote for their chosen candidate. It seemed like a good idea, but it didn't work because in Navajo culture blue was a good colour and red bad. The result was to load the dice for some candidates as against the others. Nowadays photographs are used on the ballots. [24]

Have a think about what black might signify in your culture.

Carla was shocked when Munya first invited her to think about this. It was a harsh realisation for her about how often she had used the word black to describe something that was scary or otherwise considered negative.

For Aboriginal people, the colour black is not considered a negative thing but rather as a source of great pride and strength because it is the colour of their people. They do not refer to things as being 'black' to portray negativity such as black or dark humour. When referring to black comedy, it is used to refer to Aboriginal comedy that is positive rather than negative. Nor is black the colour of death or mourning but rather the opposite colour of white like many Asian and Buddhist cultures.

When someone does not say 'please' or 'thank you', my first response is…

That's rude. No Manners. It's my children!

All the above could be true or not.

---

[24] Edward Hall, *The Silent Language*, p. 108.

Did you know there are no words for 'please' or 'thank you' in any Aboriginal language? In Torres Strait Islander languages, there is.

People often think that culture is something that just fell out of the sky. They don't see culture and language as developing out of social practices and that there are logical reasons for doing what we do. We always ask participants, "Why do you think Aboriginal languages never developed words for 'please' and 'thank you'?" After doing the kinship activity outlined in the next chapter (Chapter 5), they soon realise it has to do with *reciprocity* – the practice of exchanging things with others for mutual benefit. In cultures where there is a high degree of reciprocity where everyone is obligated to someone else, words like 'please' and 'thank you' become superfluous. So even where Aboriginal people speak English, they often don't say these words because they were never part of their culture. This doesn't mean that Aboriginal people aren't grateful. It's just that there are other ways of showing gratitude besides saying those specific words.

In Aboriginal languages, there are no words for please or thank you

Shaking hands in my culture means....

Greetings. Agreement.

All the above could be true...or not...

Did you know that in western cultures the handshake developed as a symbol of peace to show you didn't intend to harm the other person? It came from a period when people carried swords. To show they meant no harm, upon greeting another person, they simply left the sword in their scabbard as they extended their hand to shake. Gradually over time, people no longer carried swords, but the tradition of extending one's hand remained. Eventually, the reason for doing this as a form of greeting was forgotten and people assumed that it was always the case.

The handshake is a classic example of how culture evolves. In some cultures, for example, men and women do not shake hands. In Australia, men and women only started shaking hands in the 70s, and both Carla and Munya still recall hand shaking being a bit awkward in a business setting in the late 80s. Be that as it may, handshaking continues to evolve as seen by the myriad forms and variations of handshakes we see today from high fives to all sorts of complicated finger and hand tapping gestures. With the coronavirus pandemic, we have observed no handshaking or in some instances the 'elbow bump' to replace the handshake.

Shaking hands is not a traditional form of greeting in Indigenous cultures and is a recent cultural phenomenon. It is something Indigenous people have learned to do when interacting with gudia. While urban Indigenous people may be comfortable with handshakes, the more remote they are, the less comfortable they are. Some Indigenous people have pointed out it is a common greeting during Sorry Business where people shake hands as a mark of respect. But once again, it is not the firm, robust type of handshake one would expect in the wider Australian community. It is limper and a gentle shake. Generally speaking, men and women don't tend to shake hands with the opposite sex, as in Muslim cultures. If you're not confident of what to do, the best approach is always to follow someone's lead as in the adage, "When in Rome…"

Aboriginal English Versus Indigenous Languages

Did you know that about 250 Indigenous languages were spoken in Australia at the time Europeans arrived? These languages had extensive vocabularies and complex grammars. Today only a few are commonly spoken daily. But although many Aboriginal people speak English, you need to be aware that many speak a creolised version called 'Aboriginal English'. This is not pidgin or uneducated English but a distinct language in its own right.

Aboriginal English is a distinct form of English in its own right.

There are subtle differences and words or phrases can have a completely different meaning or the exact opposite. For example, the word 'deadly' in standard Australian English (SAE) usually means something dangerous whereas in Aboriginal English, it means 'fantastic, awesome, great.' In a medical context, not understanding the difference can have drastic consequences. We often say to medical practitioners don't refer to diabetes, cancer or heart disease as being 'deadly'. That's like saying to Aboriginal people, that's a great thing to have!

In our cultural awareness training we take participants through many examples where miscommunication can arise because of the different meanings of certain words and phrases such as 'broken down by sex'. Very often, gudia organisations are keen to gather gender-specific information and use the word sex instead of *men's business* and *women's business* to indicate gender. Aboriginal people only use the word sex to refer to that intimate, physical act between two people and is rarely used to indicate gender.

Even the term 'mob' can be problematic. We saw for instance in Chapter 2 that it's perfectly okay to use the word mob when referring to Indigenous people. Translating that to the use of forms however has created comedic miscommunication. For example, one organisation had forms seeking staff details such as their names, addresses and contact details, including their 'mob'. This was short-hand for mobile, but you can imagine how Aboriginal people responded. Instead of writing their *mobile* numbers they had written their tribe or nation names! This resulted in the organisation changing their forms to avoid any miscommunication. The biggest tip is to use plain and simple English and avoid:

- acronyms such as ATSI people, ABN, TFN and so on
- clichés and sporting analogies such as give me a 'ballpark figure'

- government-speak such as leverage, push back, sandpit and synergise
- technical language and jargon where possible
- Latin or other foreign phrases such as *ad hoc, quid pro quo* and so on.

In Aboriginal English, Deadly means 'fantastic, awesome, great'.

To understand what Aboriginal English sounds like, we play a skit from the Black Comedy series on ABC Television, entitled 'Black/White Woman'. It features Australian actress, Brooke Satchwell. Her character 'Tiffany' is dating an Indigenous man and wants to sound Indigenous by speaking like an Indigenous person, but she goes 'proper' overboard!

Participants are asked to try and identify as many Aboriginal English words and phrases as they can. The skit also serves a dual function, which introduces participants to Aboriginal or 'black humour'.

Be aware also that many Aboriginal and Torres Strait Islander people speak English with an accent. That's right. It's an Aboriginal or Torres Strait islander accent. Next time you're speaking with an Indigenous person or watching them speak on television or some other media, listen deeply and see if you can hear the difference.

If you're interested in finding out more, we highly recommend the book *Aboriginal Ways of Using English* by sociolinguist, Diana Eades.

Chapter 4 Takeaways

- Unconscious bias is learned stereotypes that are automatic, unintentional, deeply ingrained beliefs that affect our behaviour.

- Cultural baggage is a common metaphor to refer to our attitudes, beliefs, expectations, judgements and values.

- Direct questioning is not very common (or polite) in Aboriginal conversation. This can be tricky when working within Aboriginal communities. Try asking only one question at a time and don't ask compound questions.

- Silence in response to a question from someone within an Aboriginal community may mean that the person does not understand the question, does not know the answer, or may know but is not the right person to reply.

- For many Aboriginal people, silence is as much as part of communication as is talking - it can show respect, contemplation, disagreement, or to allow time to reflect and consider.

- In some communities, direct eye contact may be inappropriate and avoiding eye contact can be a sign of respect.

Action:

Download your free guide to common Aboriginal English words and their meanings at practicalreconciliation.com

CHAPTER 5

Kinship – They're All Related!
Step 5 – Kinship

One of the biggest stereotypes of Indigenous people is that 'They're all bloody related.' Except, this one's true – Aboriginal people *are* all related! In our cultural awareness training through an activity called the Skin Game, we take people through the principles of Indigenous kinship to better understand the deep Indigenous connections. All our activities are interactive and experiential to foster greater learning and to deal with the different modalities of learning – audio, kinaesthetic, visual and auditory. In the Skin Game, participants are assigned to Aboriginal Skin Groups from which they are tasked to find their *kantrimin* or relatives. What ensues is tremendous learning in an environment where there is much laughter and frivolity as people run around trying to find their husbands, wives, mothers and fathers and their children.

They're All Bloody Related

Kinship Structures

In Aboriginal Australia, whole tribes or nations are divided into kinship groups. The three main types of class system are "Moieties, which distinguish two classes; Sections, that distinguish four; and

Subsections, distinguishing eight." [25] The word moiety means 'half' in French. So, in moiety systems, everything is divided into two halves, including people and the environment. Like other binary divisions such as male and female, moieties complement and mirror each other. Like Yin and Yang, the objective is to achieve balance, harmony and wholeness for the whole tribe or nation. [26]

Moieties determine community governance – who is responsible for certain overall responsibilities to do with ceremonies and other community business. So, for example, among the Yolngu and their two moiety divisions, Dhuwa and Yirritja, one group oversees Love Magic and conception while the other is responsible for Sorry Business. Dhuwa is black cockatoo whereas Yirritja is white cockatoo. [27] Among the Wandjina tribes of the Kimberley, their two moieties are the Red Paint mob versus the White Paint mob, which refers to ochre colours used in Law Business. In this context, 'paint' is a sacred word as is the act of painting oneself to prepare for ceremony.

The colours red and white have special meaning relating to one's group identity. In Victoria among the Wurundjeri, the moiety divisions are Bunjil (Eagle) and Waa (Crow). Leading linguist, Robert Dixon tells us early gudia attempts to understand what this meant in practice failed dismally. For instance, the Reverend John Matthew in his book *Eaglehawk and Crow* (1899) mistakenly thought "that Aboriginal Australians were a blending of two original races, one darker skinned than the other." [28] When we play the Skin Game in our cultural awareness training, some participants continue to make the same mistake as Matthew in assuming that

---

[25] William B. McGregor, *The Languages of the Kimberley, Western Australia*, p. 51.
[26] See http://livingknowledge.anu.edu.au/learningsites/seacountry/03_moieties.htm
[27] Ibid.
[28] R.M.W. Dixon, *The Languages of Australia*, p. 15.

'skin' refers to skin *colour*. It does not. It is an Aboriginal English term that describes kinship. We love the play on words and think it fascinating that kinship contains the word *skin*. How serendipitous!

Like skin groups, you can only marry people in the *opposite* moiety. Siblings share the same moiety, so to marry each other is tantamount to incest. These 'wrong way' relationships are also described as 'poison'. They are one of several taboo relationships.

Moieties are an overarching kinship structure that houses tribal clans. So, for instance, in Yolngu kinship, there are 20 clans under each moiety. Yolngu also describe their clans as skin groups, so they effectively have 40 skin groups. [29] The algorithms in Aboriginal kinship systems are not only staggering but a mathematician's playground.

What are Skin Groups?

Skin groups refer to the subsection system. The term 'skin' is used mainly across northern Australia, but the concept is understood among all nations. In New South Wales, the term 'meat' was used in the same context. [30] As Yuin Elder, Uncle Max Dulumunmun Harrison explains, his mother would ask visitors, "What's your *gnulli*?" Gnulli means 'meat' which means your skin or skin name. [31] Ultimately, all nations operated under one kinship form or another, which were called by various names.

---

[29] See http://livingknowledge.anu.edu.au/learningsites/seacountry/04_kinship.htm
[30] Deborah Bird Rose, *Nourishing Terrains*, p. 7.
[31] Max Dulumunmun Harrison, *My People's Dreaming*, p. 92.

Where does the Term 'Skin' come from and what does it Mean?

Skin is all about identity and belonging. When people know their skin names, they understand their Dreamings and their connection to Country through stories and ceremony. It is worn proudly as a badge, and when people perform corroboree (Aboriginal dance ceremony) and partake in ceremony, they proudly display their skin or family emblem painted on their bodies. Like Scottish tartan, the different designs let people know which clan you belong to, hence the Aboriginal English term 'skin'. And as we just saw, it refers to family and connection to one another.

Kukutja Skin Group

The system Evolve shares is that of the Gugadja (Kukutja) people of the Kimberley region of Western Australia, largely because it is in the public domain and accessible through the publication *Tjarany Roughtail: The Dreaming of the Roughtail and Other Stories*. Therefore, it is not secret-sacred knowledge that is restricted. We have turned this information into a fun, interactive game taking it off the anthropology shelf. Kukutja or Gugadja country centres around Lake Gregory and the communities of Bililuna and Balgo where people speak the Kukutja language.

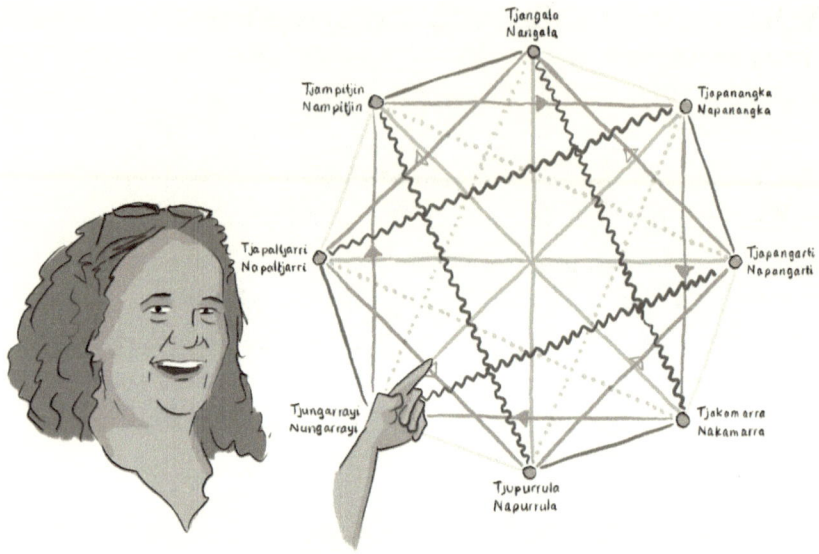

Munya explaining the Kukatja Skin System

There are eight skin groups in the Kukutja system. Each skin group has two divisions with separate skin names indicating gender. So, for instance, all the male skin names begin with Tj, which are pronounced as Dj. Thus, Tjangala becomes Djangala and so on. All female skin names begin with N.

Figure 1. Kukatja skin names depicting gender

Male	Female
Tjampitjin	Nampitjin
Tjapaltjarri	Napaltjarri
Tjungarrayi	Nungarrayi

Tjupurrula	Napurrula
Tjakamarra	Nakamarra
Tjapangarti	Napangarti
Tjapanangka	Napanganka
Tjangala	Nangala

The entire skin groups are set out in a geometric configuration resembling a star or Mandala as seen in the image of Munya explaining the Kukutja system. The basic idea is that people can only marry one other skin group, which is the opposite skin from yours. Kukutja do allow for one additional skin group you can also marry, which is a cross-cousin relationship (non-biological) but that soon becomes complicated, so we'll keep it simple for the purpose of the exercise.

How do People get their Skin?

In the Kukutja skin system, people inherit their skin names from their mother. So, ultimately this system is matriarchal. In other skin systems, people are given skin names through their father, which would be patriarchal. This system is like the Jewish tradition, which maintains that you can only claim to be Jewish if you have a Jewish mother, not Jewish father. This explains why American actress Gwyneth Paltrow doesn't claim to be Jewish even though she has a Jewish father. [32] In this regard, we say they are *same same*.

A child can never have the same skin name as their mother or father. When participants find their relatives during the Skin Game, they soon realise that the skin names return every third generation so

---

[32] Her father was American film producer-director, Bruce Paltrow.

that grandparents share the same skin name according to gender. This explains the contemporary tradition of Aboriginal grandparents referring to their grandchildren as their 'grannies'. By the same reckoning, Aboriginal aunties will refer to their nieces as 'mum' and vice versa because what mainstream Australians call aunt and uncle are mum and dad in Aboriginal culture. This is because under Aboriginal kinship, you can have many mothers and fathers as we have already seen.

Big Mob of Relatives

If you've ever spent time with Aboriginal people, it soon becomes obvious that there are so many relatives. In fact, there is not one but many mothers and fathers – not to mention numerous aunties and uncles, brothers, sisters, grandparents and so on. So why are there so many grandmothers, grandfathers, mothers, fathers, brothers, sisters, aunties, uncles and cousins? Skin provides the answer.

Under the kinship system, everyone is interrelated and interconnected. There are no outsiders. Everyone belongs. The whole tribe or nation slots into one of these skin groups, so that if your grandmother is a *Nakamarra* woman, then all the other women who fall into that skin group are also your grandmothers. If your grandfather is *Tjakamarra*, then all the other men who belong to that skin group are also your grandfather. The same goes for all the other skin groups. This kinship system is referred to as classificatory, meaning that kinship is not just biological but social. Of course, people know who their biological relatives are but the practice of referring to other people by kinship terms is about extending kinship to create closer ties with everyone else in that tribe. Kinship is also extended beyond humans to the entire Universe, including the animal world, plants and even non-animate objects such as land, stars, stones and water.

Big Mob of Relatives

In Aboriginal spiritual beliefs there is no such thing as 'non-animate' objects because everything is alive and imbued with the essence of creation. Thus, land or country is viewed as family. So too are stones, stars and water. What is more, these objects are also classified according to skin and are included in the skin system. Thus, a tree may be someone's sister or mother-in-law, a crow or eagle may be someone's brother and so on. Native Americans have a similar philosophy where they see everyone as being related to one another.

And All My Relations

The idea that we are more intimately connected or related to our fellow creatures (and the universe in which we live) is a central precept of many Indigenous cultures. It is beautifully expressed in the totemic nature of Aboriginal Dreamtime and Native American spirituality. For example, the Lakota Sioux end all their prayers with the phrase Mitakuye Oyasin "all my relations" to acknowledge our kinship and interrelatedness with all living beings with whom we share a common ancestry and destiny. [33]

Skin groups also determine group or family Dreamings. So, one group may call themselves Bat people, Crocodile mob or Possum people and so on. When an Aboriginal person speaks of their Kangaroo Dreaming for instance, they are trying to convey a profound, intimate connection they feel with that animal deep within the recesses of their soul and their consciousness. That kangaroo may be an Elder, teacher, mother, father, brother, sister, son or daughter and as one might expect with any family there is a deep, abiding sense of community with all the nuances that relationship entails. This inexplicable feeling of kindredness that Indigenous peoples feel towards their fellow creatures transcends the confines of western science with its limited understanding of what constitutes 'knowledge'.

The Mother-in-Law Taboo

Apart from bringing people together by creating close ties among everyone in the one community, skin serves several important

---

[33] Ibid, p. 99.

functions. It provides a cultural framework that sets out people's ethical and social obligations to one another. It provides a moral compass for people where the rules governing proper conduct is clearly outlined. It also serves as an in-built conflict resolution model whereby certain dynamics are curtailed such as that between a mother-in-law and her child's spouse.

Avoidance relationships are a common feature of Aboriginal cultures, which are often described as 'poison'. The strongest of these is the mother-in-law relationship, where people are forbidden from speaking or interacting with their mother-in-laws. The way that they do is usually through a third party or in instances where this isn't possible they may do so through speaking a special mother-in-law language. [34] A son-in-law or daughter-in-law does not look their mother-in-law in the eye and will often sit with their backs to each other as a mark of respect. In short, people do not experience problems with their mother-in-law because they don't talk to each other. A mother-in-law is not allowed to criticise you in any way, certainly not to your face, nor can she tell you what to do, for example, how to raise her grandchildren or treat her son or daughter. Aboriginal culture has been around for a long, long time and has a great understanding of human dynamics!

Why is there a Taboo?

When people find out about the mother-in-law taboo, they are naturally curious how and why this came about. They soon learn the Skin system is all about genetics and keeping the bloodlines pure in a small society. Anthropologists say the taboo is another way of preventing inappropriate relationships because of arranged or promised marriage where a much younger woman was promised to an older man, usually the same generation as the girl's mother.

---

[34] Ibid, pp. 93-94.

While there may be some truth to this, the real reason is all about respect as Native American authors, Russell Means and Bayard Johnson suggest. In their culture, they also share the same taboo against in-laws talking and interacting with one another. They argue that the relationship between mother and child is so special, over and above the relationship between father and child or any other being that "no-body interrupts that special relationship between the mother and child." They say, "That's why in-laws do not talk to their mothers-n-law, and vice versa." [35]

Parental Roles and Child Discipline

Generally, extended families tend to offer more support and benefits to people than nuclear families. This is because there are shared resources and more people to assist with certain duties and tasks. One notable benefit involves child-rearing. Unlike nuclear or single parent families, in Aboriginal culture child rearing and discipline is not the sole responsibility of parents. Many relatives play a major role in raising children, thus relieving parents of their parental burden. It embodies the well-known maxim, "It takes a village to raise a child."

Each person within the kinship system has a specific role to play in child rearing. Fathers are responsible for supplying families with food while mothers are responsible for feeding and nurturing her child. But that's where their primary responsibilities end. All other family members are responsible for guidance, teaching and ceremonial matters, including spiritual guidance and initiation of boys and girls into becoming young men and women. Generally, the child's aunt and uncle are responsible for their initiation and spiritual guidance.

---

[35] Russell Means & Bayard Johnson, *If You've Forgotten The Names of the Clouds, You've Lost Your Way*, at Location 375-380 Kindle.

But grandparents also play a special role in spiritual teachings such as the Wudu fires, [36] which take place at dawn and sunset. Here the child learns about social rules to do with self-respect and respecting others. So far as disciplining children is concerned both the uncles and aunties can chastise children and teach them right from wrong. Rarely does the mother or father get involved so they can concentrate on being the good cop instead of the stroppy parent.

So, What do you Call your Grandmother?

When we play the Skin Game, people want to know things like, "What is the Aboriginal word for grandmother?" Our first response is, in which language? (There are only about 120 or so to choose from). Our second response is, "Which one? Maternal grandmother or paternal grandmother?" English speakers are stumped by this because they aren't aware of this cultural distinction. People from an Italian or other European background or people who speak a language other than English, on the other hand, are more attuned to this.

Like Italian, most Aboriginal languages have four sets of kinship terms for grandparents to indicate their relationship to one's parents. In other words, whether the grandparent is on the mother's or father's side. For example, in Bardi, the maternal grandmother (on Mother's side) is *Garminy* whereas the paternal grandmother (on Father's side) is *Golli*. By the same token, the maternal grandfather is *Nyumi* and the paternal grandfather is *Galoonoordoo* or *Gooloo* for short. Some people have suggested that the Australian tendency to shorten English words like 'arvo' for afternoon or 'brekky' for breakfast is because of our influence.

In Kukutja, the maternal grandmother is *Kaparli* and the maternal grandfather is *Tjamu*. The paternal grandmother is *Ngawawtji* and the paternal grandfather is *Kirlaki*. Curiously, the word for father in

---
[36] David Mowarljarlai & Jutta Malnic, *Yorro Yorro*, p. 105.

the Kukutja language is *Mama*! All in all, Kukutja has 22 kinship terms, excluding Aboriginal English terms like cousin-brother and cousin-sister.

Different terms for mother-in-law are used depending on whether the person who is speaking is male or female. So, for instance, men call their mother-in-law *Yumari*, which is the same term for son-in-law. Women on the other hand, call their mother-in-law *Nyungarri*, which is also the term for daughter-in-law.

In Kukutja, husbands and wives have the same common term for spouse, which is *Nyupa*. And if the letters r-r-a is added to the word as in *Nyuparra*, this becomes the term for marriage. So, the skin system is also known as the marriage system because it determines who can marry whom. The preferred marriage partner is always of the opposite skin group and in Aboriginal English is referred to as who you are 'straight' for. It has nothing to do with sexuality but rather the lines that are drawn illustrating the proper marriage partner.

In one of our cultural awareness training workshops, Munya made the mistake of asking one man, Neville, who he was straight for. With hand on hip and a petulant pose he cried, "I'm not *straight* for anyone." The room howled with laughter. Once Munya explained it wasn't about sexuality, he played the game and loved it.

When people play the Skin Game, it soon becomes obvious that Aboriginal skin is all about inclusivity. Gays, lesbian and transgender people are included in the system. Traditionally Aboriginal people were not homophobic. These negative, limiting views have largely been imported through religious beliefs and convictions that are non-Indigenous. This is not to say that homophobia is not present in Aboriginal culture today. We are simply stating the traditional case.

Other Kinship Terms

The other amazing thing about Aboriginal languages is that there are additional words for certain relationships that have no equivalent words to describe them in English. For example, the English term 'orphan' generally describes a child who has lost both parents rather than just one. Aboriginal languages on the other hand are far more specific. For example, there are terms to describe a *parent* who has lost a child as opposed to the other way around. So, in Dyirbal a mother who has lost a child is *mangguy* and a father who has lost a child is *murrgabi*. Moreover, a child who has lost its mother is called *wulunggulaa* whereas a child who has lost its father is *dungun*. [37]

For Aboriginal and Torres Strait Islander people, it is all about relationships and how we relate to one another. There are even words to describe people that share the same name. For example, back home we refer to someone with the same name as *goombarli*. Indigenous people see family in all that they see, do and hear.

Skin Birds and Mother-in-Law Trees

Because the Dreaming is so profound and prolific, everything in nature is a lesson to be taught and learned. The environment plays such a crucial role in teaching Indigenous people of their culture. People single out the multi-coloured Blue Mountain parrot as a warning to people of what happens when you marry 'wrong way' or go with someone who is not the right skin for you - with your skin getting all mixed up. This shows Aboriginal people had a good knowledge of genetics and the medical complications that arise from marrying close relatives such as your siblings or first cousins.

---

[37] R.M.W Dixon, *Australia's Original Languages*, p. 48.

Blue Mountain Parrot or Skin Bird

In the Kimberley where Munya comes from, there are mother-in-law trees called Jigal (*Lysiphyllum cunninghamii*). It serves as a teaching aide about the Skin system and is a visual reminder of the mother-in-law taboo. If you look closely at the tree's leaves, you will see that they are facing away from each other as is the proper behaviour for mother-in-laws.

Carla & Talise Rogers with Danika Newton
beside the Mother-in-Law Tree

Can Non-Aboriginal People be given Skin Names?

If you've ever worked in an Aboriginal community, however remote, chances are you have or will be given a skin name. Sometimes when we play the Skin Game some people will tell us they already have one and if translatable or compatible, we slot them into the appropriate group. So, the short answer is yes, non-Aboriginal people can be given skin names. When this happens, you are then adopted into the kinship network and expected to fulfil your Skin obligations, which will have an impact on your work relationships within that community. Although Aboriginal people don't expect gudia (a non-Indigenous person) to have the same level of knowledge about cultural knowledge, matters and protocols, nonetheless you need to be aware of some potential areas of conflict. This includes being aware of avoidance relationships such as the Mother-in-Law taboo or other 'poison' relationships.

If you are a health professional or medical practitioner for example, there may be restrictions in treating or communicating with a patient because of kinship obligations. This can also extend to giving evidence in a legal situation, which will have to be clearly thought out in the tendering of evidence in a court of law. When giving medical and legal advice, you will find that the whole family expects to be given information. This does have ramifications for western concepts of privacy requirements being imposed on Aboriginal families and may require you to modify these.

Kinship obligations may also extend to law business, including ceremony obligations. You may decline the offer of a skin name if you feel you lack the cultural nous and confidence to fulfil your kinship obligations, but you need to handle this with great diplomacy less you cause offence. Should you find yourself in this situation, we suggest you seek advice from a learned community member.

How is Skin Relevant Today?

Some people think skin is no longer relevant, but it still plays a major role in how Aboriginal people relate to each other, even in cities or other urban areas or where whole systems have been demolished through colonisation. This is because the community values that underpin the skin system still live on – values of belonging, relationship and reciprocity for example. In places where the original, traditional skin names may no longer be because of language loss, you still find Aboriginal people relating to each other along skin lines. So, while the traditional names for grandmother, grandfather, mother and father and so on may have been lost, they are simply replaced by English terms such as bro (brother), tidda (sister), cuz (cousin), uncle and aunt and so on. Indeed, uncle and aunt are terms of respect for Elders in the community or for older people generally. This in turn raises the question of who is an Elder, something we often get asked in our cultural awareness training.

Who are Elders?

People often think that just because someone is referred to as Uncle or Aunty that it automatically means they are considered an Elder. But this is not necessarily the case. Often the term Uncle or Aunty are used to show respect to an older person in the community. An Elder on the other hand, is someone who holds high cultural and spiritual knowledge. Munya has a saying, "All Elders are Aunties and Uncles but not all Aunties and Uncles are Elders." [38] Hopefully that makes it easier to understand the difference.

Sorry Business

The other way in which skin is still relevant today relates to Sorry Business. This is the Aboriginal English word to describe death and funerals. When a death has taken place in the community it is referred to as Sorry Business. You may have an Aboriginal workmate who you notice isn't at work. When you enquire why they're absent, someone may say that they're off on Sorry Business. Knowing what that means, your next question may be, "Oh, who's died?" Then a colleague might say, "Oh, I think it was her grandmother." So, you begin to think, "That's odd. I'm sure her grandmother died three months ago." And it may well be that her biological grandmother did die but what about all the other women she calls grandmother? If they die, your colleague is socially obligated to show up at her funeral just as she would her biological grandmother.

Now that you have seen that there are many mothers, fathers, grandparents and other relatives, you can see that there are many funerals in Aboriginal culture due to kinship. This compounded with the fact of low life expectancy among Indigenous people means that deaths occur more frequently than in the average Australian's lifetime.

---

[38] Munya Andrews, *Journey Into Dreamtime*, p. 98.

Practical Reconciliation

When an Aboriginal person is dying, be prepared for many people dropping by to visit and pay their respects. Given the big mob of relatives, the home or hospital where someone is dying can get crowded as a result. The essential point to bear in mind is that Sorry Business affects everyone in the community and when a member dies, everyone will mourn their death. People will travel far and wide to attend Sorry Business, no matter the distance. In some of the nations, Sorry Business activities are the responsibility of certain skin groups and individuals.

Work Relationships

Skin will also play a part in an Indigenous person's work relationships. Their workplace may have to develop and implement special measures for dealing with kin relationships, especially protocols in dealing with staff members who are in poison or avoidance relationships such as mother-in-laws.

How does an organisation deal with these relationships in the workplace? You may have staff members who can't speak or interact with each other because of skin obligations. Some organisations have special rules whereby one mother-in-law will enter work through the front door, while the other will enter via the back door. Some people may consider this to be an unequal thing whereas to Aboriginal people it doesn't matter because they don't place a premium on whether the door is at the front or at the rear. Some organisations have erected partitions between Aboriginal staff members in avoidance relationships who are on the same work team. The extent to which an organisation can cater to these cultural requirements is of course, highly dependent on adequate resources, including budgetary constraints and political considerations. The real question is to what extent organisations value their Indigenous workers and whether they are committed to Indigenous retention, because skin is something to be seriously considered in these matters.

Kinship Today

We saw that skin is still relevant to Aboriginal people in various ways. The crucial point is that even though cultures inevitably change and evolve, nonetheless some of what makes that culture intrinsically Aboriginal or Torres Strait Islander will remain as fertile as the ground from which the culture draws upon. We have seen for instance that where colonisation has had a devastating impact on Aboriginal people and their society, Aboriginal people still follow the old ways, including skin, even where English has replaced traditional languages.

What this reveals is the importance of Indigenous cultural frameworks in keeping culture alive in the face of enormous change. Therefore, in his song about the Stolen Generations *Took the Children Away*, Koori singer-songwriter, Archie Roach proudly proclaims at the song's end that, 'The children came back.' This powerful refrain is testament to Aboriginal cultural resilience that celebrates the strength of Aboriginal family ties and the strong sense of belonging and connection they feel to the land and each other. It flies in the face of assimilation policies and practices designed to rid Aboriginal people of their cultural identity and birthright.

Chapter 5 Takeaways

- There are three main types of kinship schemes – *Moieties*, which distinguish two classes; *Sections*, that distinguish four; and *Subsections* (skin), distinguishing eight.

- The term skin is used mainly across northern Australia, but the concept is understood elsewhere among other tribes or nations.

- Skin is all about identity and belonging. When people know their skin names, they understand their Dreamings and their connection to Country through stories and ceremony.

- There are eight skin groups in the Kukutja system. Each skin group is made up of two divisions with separate skin names indicating gender (e.g. Tjakamarra and Nakamarra).

- Under the kinship system, everyone is interrelated and interconnected. There are no outsiders. Everyone belongs.

- Avoidance relationships are a common feature of Aboriginal cultures, which are often described as 'poison' or 'wrong-way'.

- Generally, extended families tend to offer more support and benefits to people than nuclear families. This is because there are shared resources and more people to assist with certain duties and tasks.

- An Elder is someone who holds high cultural and spiritual knowledge.

- Sorry Business is the Aboriginal English word to describe death, dying and funerals.

> **Action:**
>
> Watch a video of Aunty Munya explaining the Kukatja Skin System, at practicalreconciliation.com

CHAPTER 6

Closing the Privilege Gap
Step 6 - Privilege

For more than a decade, the popular catch-all slogan 'Closing the Gap' became a convenient phrase to highlight Indigenous disadvantage. Essentially, the gap refers to the huge social and economic gap that exists between Indigenous and non-Indigenous Australians. Despite a well-intentioned government strategy, the truth is that the gap remains.

Outcomes for Indigenous and non-Indigenous Australians are currently miles apart. No matter how the government decides to act, the responsibility to help close this gap rests on the shoulders of each one of us. Having read this far, we know you are up to the task. Let us not forget the power of one. Individuals can and do make a positive difference.

What is the Gap?

On the 20th of March 2008, the historic 'Closing the Gap' agreement was signed between the federal and state governments to work together to eliminate the difference in life expectancy and other outcomes between Indigenous and non-Indigenous Australians. This inequality includes shorter life expectancy, higher rates of infant mortality, poorer health including malnutrition and hospitalisation for chronic diseases, suicide rates double that of the rest of Australia, higher rates of incarceration and lower levels of education and employment. While some progress was made during the decade (only three of the initial six targets were achieved) a large gap remains - in education, employment, health, justice and life expectancy (some of which weren't selected as key targets such as employment and justice).

So Why is There Still a Large Gap?

To date, there has been no official evaluation of the Closing the Gap policy and strategy. Some critics have argued the Government bit off more than it could chew – that the net was cast far too wide, that perhaps they might have achieved more with sizable chunks of government reform and targets.

Reconciliation Australia has taken a broader view of race relations as contributing to the gap that exists. [39] In researching people's attitudes they've shown that we still have a long way to go to reduce racism, nurture stronger relationships, build trust and develop a culture of respect between Indigenous and non-Indigenous Australians. There are clear indicators that we are moving in the right direction, albeit slowly. Specifically, between 2014 and 2018, while:

- Only 37% of Australians either *occasionally or regularly socialised with Aboriginal or Torres Strait Islander Australians*, engagement grew by 7%.

- 51% of Indigenous Australians agreed that *Australia is a racist country* and 38% of non-Indigenous Australians, both communities have become *more positive about the possibility of unity.*

- 43% of Aboriginal or Torres Strait Islander Australians *experienced at least one form of racial prejudice in the last six months* (including verbal abuse, refusal of entry to a venue or physical violence), compared to 20% of non-Indigenous Australians – Indigenous respondents reported a small but steady decline in their responses for very high and fairly high prejudice between Indigenous and non-Indigenous Australians.

Unfortunately, the picture painted for some areas was grimmer, with the situation worsening between 2014 and 2018. n 2018, a

---

[39] See "The State of Reconciliation in Australia: Our History, Our Story, Our Future", *Reconciliation Australia*, 2018.

smaller proportion of Aboriginal or Torres Strait Islander Australians felt ***culturally empowered*** when compared with non-Indigenous Australians. 19% of Indigenous Australians reported that they could ***never be themselves at work*** (up from 10% in 2016). 25% said they could ***never be themselves in their interactions with law and order*** - up from 16% in 2016. [40]

There is still a long way to go to reduce prejudice, improve relationships and achieve reconciliation. While many of these results show that we are moving in the right direction, the treatment (the 'booing campaign') of our 2014 Australian of the Year Adam Goodes, causes great pause and sorrow. We hope that all Australians can watch either *The Final Quarter* or *The Australian Dream* documentaries that explore the issue.

In terms of equality and equity, recognition of the rights of Indigenous Australians and respect for the distinctive collective cultures of Aboriginal and Torres Strait Islander peoples are key. The results in Reconciliation Australia's 2018 Australian Reconciliation Barometer (ARB) report [41] show that we still have a long way to go to close the gap in key areas of disadvantage, namely education, health, employment and justice. Specifically, in 2018:

- Only 48% of Aboriginal and Torres Strait Islanders considered their living conditions to be comfortable when compared to 65% of non-Indigenous Australians. This gap has widened by 6% since 2016. How has this happened?

- A greater proportion of Indigenous respondents (45%) believed that the Australian education system did not prepare children well for employment when compared to non-Indigenous Australians (40%).

---

[40] Ibid.

[41] See https://www.reconciliation.org.au/wp-content/uploads/2019/02/final_full_arb-full-report-2018.pdf

Any Australian's life choices, opportunities and future should not be determined by the colour of his or her skin. A reconciled Australia is the ultimate goal – a fair, equal society where all Australians share the same opportunities.

For all of us to make a difference, understanding the gap is a great first step. The next step, which can be more confronting, is to understand the role that privilege plays in creating and widening the gap.

What has Privilege got to do with it?

Let's tackle the hard question first – what is privilege?

Exploring privilege can be uncomfortable but it's important to be mindful that some of our greatest insights and learning come when we are pushed out of our comfort zones. You have no choice where you are born or who your parents and family are. However, that lottery can mean that there are some things in life that you'll not experience. There are also some opportunities or advantages that you will get that others don't just because of who you are. And with privilege, there will be things that never cross your mind. In her novel *Small Great Things*, Jodi Picoult explores racism and privilege in America that is equally relevant to Australia. She says:

> "When I was researching this book, I asked white mothers how often they talk about racism with their children. Some said occasionally; some admitted they never discussed it. When I asked the same question of black mothers, they all said, every day. I've come to see that ignorance is a privilege, too." [42]

Being privileged doesn't mean you haven't had a hard life or tough experiences, and that you've never had to struggle, or face disadvantage

---
[42] Jodi Picoult, *Small Great Things*, p. 463.

or discrimination (and by the same token it doesn't mean that a person less privileged hasn't worked hard either).

What matters is what we do or don't do with our privilege.

Picoult chose the title of her book from a quote by Martin Luther King, "If I cannot do great things, I can do small things in a great way." This chapter is largely about the small things we can do in a great way.

Closing the Privilege Gap - with the Privilege Walk

> "Don't say I don't even notice race like it's a positive thing. Instead, recognise that differences between people make it harder for some to cross a finish line, and create fair paths to success for everyone that accommodate those differences." [43]

To explore the role of privilege in Indigenous disadvantage, we use an exercise called the Privilege Walk. This activity is designed to explore the underlying privileges that certain individuals or groups of people not only enjoy but are rewarded in society for no other reason than their gender, ethnicity, nationality or their sexuality. The exercise provides a visual illustration of the concept of white privilege which American writer Peggy McIntosh wrote about in her seminal essay, "White Privilege: Unpacking the Invisible Knapsack" in 1988. [44] McIntosh highlights advantages as far ranging from getting a promotion without someone suspecting that it was due to your skin colour to buying dolls, toys and children's books that feature people of your ethnicity.

---

[43] Ibid.
[44] "White Privilege: Unpacking the Invisible Knapsack" first appeared in *Peace and Freedom Magazine*, July/August 1989, pp. 10-12, a publication of the Women's International League for Peace and Freedom, Philadelphia, PA.

When we first began doing the privilege walk in our cultural awareness programs to demonstrate the gap, there was some initial resistance and concern. But once we explained our rationale for including it, it has proved an effective tool in raising consciousness and awareness of privilege in all its various forms and its negative impact on certain groups of people.

We have adapted the Privilege Walk to Australian society to explore the hidden and apparent privileges of 'white' Australians in relation to the disadvantages of Aboriginal and Torres Strait Islander peoples – the Indigenous peoples of Australia.

Doing the Privilege Walk in Evolve's
Cultural Awareness Workshops

The purpose of the Privilege Walk is to learn to recognise how power and privilege can affect our lives even when we are not aware it is happening. It is not intended to belittle, ridicule or make anyone feel guilty or ashamed of his or her privilege or lack thereof. Rather, it seeks to demonstrate the hidden power of privilege and the ways in which it serves to disempower and disadvantage certain individuals or groups of people in society. The exercise is revelatory in the sense that it shows that everyone enjoys privileges of some kind one way or the other, albeit in different shades and degrees. By revealing our various privileges, we can begin to see ways in which we can use our individual and collective privileges to work for social justice. It is not about blaming anyone for having more power or privilege in society or for receiving more help in achieving certain goals, but to have an opportunity to identify both obstacles and benefits experienced in our lives.

The kinds of things that we ask you to reflect on in the Privilege Walk include:

- If you can go shopping and feel confident that you're not going to be followed by suspicious staff because of the way you look
- If most of your teachers shared your ethnicity or cultural background
- Whether your parents attended university
- If you're a woman; or
- If any member of your family was removed as a part of the Stolen Generation.

Talking about privilege is not an easy thing to do because of our different political views and ideology. But after doing the Privilege Walk, people begin to see how people are impacted by the different lives that we lead – that there are some things in life that many of us don't have to think about or experience. Like being followed by suspicious staff in a store. After doing the Privilege Walk there is ample time to discuss and explore any issues that arise for everyone. Not everyone agrees with the activity, but at least it engenders robust discussion where people share their gained insights.

Critiquing the Privilege Walk

In critiquing the activity, some participants feel that it can shame those less privileged. Our observation is that while this might happen from time to time, less privileged people have found it empowering because it acknowledges their struggles in life and gives them a voice.

Rightly, people have also noted, especially after learning of Aboriginal kinship and the sense of belonging, that there are many cultural advantages (for example values) of being an Aboriginal or Torres Strait Islander person. While this might be true, the purpose of the exercise is to explore the privilege of those who have historically held advantages in terms of power and economic resources. In an Australian context, this refers to those from an Anglo-Christian background. Munya, who has participated in these walks hundreds of times as she is often the only Aboriginal person in the group, regularly finishes at the back of the group, behind the line everyone started on. Munya is not surprised about where she ends up, growing up Indigenous in Australia.

Knowing where you'll finish is not necessarily common. Munya has a powerful memory of a young Aboriginal woman who took part in the walk and while she expected to finish close to the front, she was surprised to end up at the back of the room. She said, "I'm young, urban and educated – I should be up there with my colleagues." This led to deeper discussion around glass ceilings and institutionalised racism that helped her better understand how privilege gets in the way by disadvantaging her.

Carla on the other hand often ends up towards the front of the group: "I think for me, to be aware of my own privilege, is the most powerful and proactive thing I can do as a non-Indigenous person. I work with Munya and a lot of Indigenous people, but I'm still learning and coming across a new privilege every week, and this has helped me grow as a person. These privileges include having parents who are in their 80s, not having to iron my daughter's clothes for fear that she will be taken away from me, having a credit card, knowing how to apply for a bank loan, basically never having to worry about if I am being discriminated against because of my skin colour".

Reflecting on Privilege

Acknowledging privilege shouldn't be threatening to those who have it because it changes depending on context. As Munya says: "When I'm walking down the street and I see a homeless person, I'm more privileged than them in that context because I have a good job and a beautiful home. It's not about feeling guilty about your privileges. You can't help the family you were born into and the advantages you got through life. It's about being aware of how those privileges disadvantage others and helping those around you."

Reflecting on her privilege as a white Australian, Carla says:

"Every day I experience an advantage or opportunity that I have that others do not enjoy just because of the colour of my skin. My learning about privilege is lifelong. A very simple example of this is having a credit card. Countless times I've been called late at night by a distressed team or community member where the hotel is refusing check-in as they do not have a credit card. Having a credit card is a privilege, as simple as that sounds. And this is where guilt and shame come in (or does not come in). Guilt or shame is the number one enemy of allyship. I have had no choice about my cultural heritage. However, I do have a choice about becoming aware of my privilege and finding out what I can do to support others who don't have the same privileges. I do have a choice to speak up and interrupt racism where I can. I do have a choice to learn from my mistakes."

Having a credit card is a privilege, as simple as that sounds

Chapter 6 Takeaways

- The Closing the Gap agreement was signed between the federal and state governments on the 20th of March 2008, to work together to eliminate the difference in life expectancy and other outcomes between Indigenous and non-Indigenous Australians.

- It is important to understand the role of privilege in creating the gap.

- Acknowledging privilege shouldn't be threatening to those who have it, because it changes depending on context.

- For equality to take place, recognising the rights of Indigenous Australians and respecting the distinctive collective cultures of Aboriginal and Torres Strait Islander peoples are key.

> **Action:**
>
> **At practicalreconciliation.com, you can:**
>
> - Download our annually updated snapshot of the Closing the Gap initiative and discussion paper on the State of Reconciliation in Australia
>
> - Take our online privilege walk

CHAPTER 7

Becoming an Ally
Step 7 - Allies

Practical Reconciliation - Becoming An Ally

At Evolve, we place a strong emphasis on providing practical tools and resources so you can make a difference. Very often we're asked, "How can I help in the Reconciliation process?" or "What can I do?". Apart from educating yourself about Indigenous people and finding out more about their cultures, challenges, and issues facing them, the good news is that you can become an ally and make a real difference.

What's an *Ally*, you say? Isn't that a wartime thing? No, that's just a very narrow reading and usage of the word. So, individuals and not just nation states can become allies to each other. Now a lot of people associate being an ally with the LGBT movement but that is not its only application. You can become an ally to any marginalised or oppressed group. In fact, that was the original intention of Re-evaluation Counselling (RC), the movement that first introduced the concept to the world. It's now been adopted by many individuals and organisations that are committed to social justice and creating a fairer and just society.

Here at Evolve, we've adopted the Allies Model to encourage people to become allies to Australia's Indigenous peoples as part of our cultural awareness training. The response we've received from participants, so far, has been nothing short of fantastic. Through this amazing tool, people's passion for justice and reconciliation is ignited as they uncover simple actions and steps that they can take to make a difference.

Who or what is an Ally?

Most people understand an Ally to be someone who supports, empowers, or stands up for another person or a group of people. Through their actions, an ally can effectively change attitudes, behaviours, policies and practices that impact marginalised groups.

I'm sure you would agree from this definition that you've been an Ally to someone or something, sometime in your life. You just didn't call it that.

Looking back on her life, Munya can recall many instances where she spoke out against someone being bullied at school or work, which explains our attraction to this model. At school, Munya took it upon herself to protect kids that were being bullied. In the cartoon below, we recommend not taking a physical approach - there are more creative and empowering ways to resolve conflict - but you get the idea.

Munya being an Ally at school

The language of Allyship

Like any movement, the Ally movement has its own special terms and jargon that serve as linguistic shorthand for its key concepts and principles. For example, the Allies Model talks about things such as interrupting racism, which is exactly what it means. You may hear or experience a racist incident at work or in the community for instance. An Ally interrupts that racist behaviour by drawing attention to it by calling it out. But there is an action component to interrupting racism that is focused on re-education – the idea that you not only call out bad behaviour, but you explain why that behaviour is unacceptable in a fair and just society.

The other thing that Allies point out is that it's not our intention that matters but rather, its impact on other people's lives. For example, the Stolen Generations policy of removing Aboriginal children from their families was justified by the Australian government at the time as doing it *For Their Own Good* as Anna Haebich writes in her book of that name. This speaks to the government's intention of their now discredited policies that failed to consider their devastating impact on the lives of Aboriginal and Torres Strait Islander people.

Thinking about the impact of our course of action before we implement them is part of risk aversion of most modern bureaucrats and organisations' best practices. Being mindful of our carbon footprint and other negative impacts as we move through the world also aligns with spiritual philosophies such as Aboriginal Dreamtime and Buddhism. Buddhism exhorts us to do no harm as we walk on this planet with our fellow human beings and other creatures. This tenet extends to the treatment of our planet and the land on which we live.

How do I become an Ally?

A good place to start is to read the movement's guidebook, *Becoming an Ally: Breaking the Cycle of Oppression in People* by Anne Bishop. It provides good background reading, including practical examples and ideas.

In our cultural awareness training, participants explore ways in which they, individually or collectively, can become Allies to Aboriginal and Torres Strait Islander people. And in this, you are only limited by your imagination.

In many instances, organisations and individuals already have amazing ways in which they are already doing this. It may be through their Reconciliation Action Plan (RAP), or special policies and programs that aim to improve the lives of Indigenous people through culturally appropriate service delivery. The objective is to come up with as many practical ideas and suggestions that are achievable. It's an incredibly empowering exercise that gets people excited about how they can make a difference.

We also share a YouTube video by Franchesca Ramsey, an African American actress/comedian who gives 'Five Tips for Being An Ally'.

Ramsey's Five Tips are:

1. Understand your Privilege

In the previous chapter and in Step 6, we explored the Privilege Walk. As Ramsey says, "A lot of people get hung up on the word privilege. Privilege does not mean that you are rich, that you've had an easy life, that everything has been handed to you and that you've never had to struggle or work hard. All it means is that there are some things in life that you will not experience or ever have to think about just because of who you are." Ramsey maintains before you can fight for the rights of others, you have to understand what rights you have and others don't. "That's privilege," she says.

2. Listen and do your homework

"You have to be willing to listen", says Ramsey. That means doing your homework and educating yourself about the issues impacting an oppressed group or minority.

3. Speak up but not over
"An Ally's job is to support", says Ramsey, "not to take over from them or take credit for things they're already saying."

4. Mistakes happen
Ramsey goes on to say, "Realise that you're gonna make mistakes and apologise when you do. Nobody's perfect. Unlearning problematic things takes time and work, so you are bound to mess up and trip and fall." But you pick yourself up, apologise and move on." She goes on to say, "Just remember, it's not about your intent, it's about your impact, so when you get called out, make sure to listen, apologise, commit to changing your behaviour and move forward."

5. Ally is a verb
Finally, Ramsey concludes with probably the most important tip of all. "Saying you're an Ally is not enough," she says, "you've got to do the work." This means, getting in there and getting your hands dirty and demonstrating your commitment to the cause.

Why should I become an Ally?

No one should ever be forced to do anything, but hopefully we can excite you enough to want to become an Ally to Aboriginal and Torres Strait Islander people. Apart from making you feel good about yourself, it will help advance the cause of Reconciliation in this nation and build a fairer society for everyone. The truth is that there are simply not enough Indigenous people to educate Australians. We need all the help we can get, especially where we find our Indigeneity being questioned and under attack. So please read and find out about this exciting, practical tool for achieving social justice and a better society or come along to our cultural awareness training to find out how you can become an Ally to our mob.

Chapter 7 Takeaways

- An Ally is someone who supports, empowers, or stands up for another person or a group of people.

- There are many ways to become an Ally, including joining formal groups or taking an informal stand on your own.

- Five practical tips for being an ally are to:
    - understand your Privilege
    - listen and do your homework
    - speak up but not over
    - acknowledge that mistakes happen
    - remember that ally is a verb – it is about taking action

- Becoming an Ally is essential to practical reconciliation because there are not enough Indigenous people to educate Australians on the need for cultural sensitivity.

Action:

What action will you take as an ally? We'd love you to let us know on our allies' ideas wall at practicalreconciliation.com

CHAPTER 8

Engagement and Cultural Protocols

Congratulations! We have covered a lot of ground together walking through the seven steps. In this chapter, we want to share with you some approaches and tips to develop meaningful relationships with Aboriginal and Torres Strait Islander peoples and communities. We look at our Songlines Pathways® approach to building relationships with communities and explore ways of meeting with large groups that are based on Indigenous cultural protocols and methods. You will find this chapter especially valuable if you are working with Aboriginal communities.

SONGLINES PATHWAYS® - ENGAGING WITH COMMUNITIES

Let's start with the big picture. How can you meaningfully engage and develop genuine relationships with Aboriginal communities? How do you build trust? We have shared with you our R3 Culture® approach (Reflect, Relate, Reconcile) which is a strategy you can use in the moment while you are having a conversation. We want to take a step back now and look at an overall approach to engagement. A map or guidebook that, like a mentor, can be by you and your team's side.

We combined our collective experience of working within communities. Through trial and error, we developed a simple approach that everyone can follow. These are the Songlines Pathways®. This engaging pathway draws deeply from Aboriginal cultural heritage and wisdom.

Songlines represent traditional trading routes across the nation where information and resources are shared. It teaches individuals and organisations the value of networking through making deep and meaningful connections with Aboriginal people and their communities.

In the Kimberley region of Western Australia for example, this vast sharing network known as Wunan is depicted in our business logo.

Wunan by Munya Andrews

While we run a full day training program on the Songlines Pathways® and it has a detailed guidebook and map, we wanted to share with you the key steps here.

The ONE Thing

If we could only tell you one thing about community engagement it would be this:

Involve those who you wish to engage with in the design of the engagement.

Or even simpler,

Ask people who you want to hear from how they would like to be involved and what will work for them.

In buzzword speak this is now known as co-design.

So how do we do this when we are engaging with hundreds or thousands of people?

We usually bring together a 'design team' made up of people including decision-makers, staff, community and leaders, from both the agency and the community, which includes anyone who:

- is interested in the project,
- may be affected by the outcomes, and

- has good networks and links with people who have similar interests.

We then meet with the design team to step through the Songlines Pathway®.

The Songlines Pathway®

What?

The first thing to do is to ask: Is this really engagement or are we just telling people about what we are doing? In other words, is the main purpose to engage or to inform? We have a simple test for this. Is what I am doing engagement? YES, if you can tick all three boxes:

- ☑ There are genuine opportunities for the community to contribute to decision-making and to affect outcomes.

- ☑ The agency still has important decisions to make and is not already committed to a specified outcome.

- ☑ The agency has clearly defined what is negotiable (on the table for discussion) and what isn't (off the table for discussion).

The last one can be tricky but especially important to do. In any engagement, it is important to manage expectations. To do this, you must be clear about what you are asking people. What can and can't be changed? The design team brainstorms this and when we have come to an agreed list, it is included in key communications messages.

If you were building a facility for example, a non-negotiable would be the building code, a negotiable would be elements of the design.

Carla has worked extensively on the management of National Parks and protected areas that are cooperatively owned and managed with Traditional Owners. So, in co-creating a management plan, a non-negotiable would be any laws that say what the plan has to deal with, or what can or can't happen in an area (for example, protecting sacred sites). A negotiable might be the types of visitor facilities provided.

Why?

A crucial first step in any engagement program is to ask why you (or the agency) are doing it. We have experienced first-hand the benefits of effective engagement which include:

- solutions that meet community needs
- community ownership and buy-in
- solutions that are understood, supported and make a difference
- an increase in trust and resilience in relationships.

So, how do you know if you have been successful? Defining your criteria for success is one of the most important things that you can do during the design of your engagement program. Some ways of doing this include:

- converting each key objective of your engagement program into a question. For example, if an objective is to enable the community to evaluate options, an evaluation question could be: "Did the community have access to adequate and timely information to enable it to make a reasoned and informed evaluation of the proposals?"
- work with your design team and ask them what success would look like. Simply, the question might be: "What

three things MUST happen for you to consider our engagement program a success?" Add these to your list of success criteria.

Who?

Aboriginal and Torres Strait Islander culture and communities are diverse and there are many different nations and groups living across Australia. A one-size-fits-all approach will not work, and we need to tailor our ways of working and communicating to meet the needs of the individuals and communities concerned. To do this, you need to do as much as you can to understand who you are engaging with and their unique needs.

Relationships, Respect, and being Yourself

Establishing good rapport and relationships with Aboriginal and Torres Strait Islander people is at the heart of all successful engagement. Often people are not sure how to do this, who to connect with and are worried about offending.

A great place to start is with respect. Our personal experience is that where you have demonstrated your respect for Aboriginal and Torres Strait Islander people and their culture, then mistakes you may make in interpersonal relationships and communication are more likely to be forgiven or overlooked by Aboriginal and Torres Strait Islander people. What is important is that you have integrity and that you are honest and respectful in your dealings.

The *Who* of the Participant (Getting the Right People Involved)

As the agency of an engagement program, there are four main steps in exploring the 'who' of the participant. They are:

1. Identifying who you want to make sure is involved (who is impacted?);
2. Asking who wants to be involved (who is interested?);
3. Seeking to understand the specific requirements of groups or individuals; and
4. Developing and choosing strategies that will attract both (1) and (2).

Remember that you are not expected to have all the answers. The beauty of having a 'design team' is that you can ASK rather than second guess who and how best to involve people. It may not be possible for you to spend extended time in Aboriginal and Torres Strait Islander communities but there is a lot you can find out before you engage.

In our training programs, we do a simple exercise to get the whole 'system' or 'community' in the room using plastic bottle tops, rocks, whatever we can find. We brainstorm who the key players are, and then using a bottle top to represent a different organisation/person/group we have a conversation to explore potential dynamics, key risks and challenges.

How we Rocked our Program

Carla

The Evolve Team was coaching two Aboriginal communities in remote northern Queensland to develop community safety plans.

Practical Reconciliation

This was a community with complex issues. They called it the 'hard yarns' - alcohol, violence, drugs, suicide. We were having our first design team workshop. I had flown in but mistakenly left the plastic bottle tops back at home on the kitchen bench. My colleague ran out to the car park and grabbed a range of rocks of different sizes. We set the rocks up on a table on top of butcher's paper, and the design team used post-it notes to identify all the key stakeholders, placing a post-it-note on top of each rock. We then had a conversation about how we were going to work together, with the team moving the rocks around to describe the different relationships.

My heart sank when they presented their final result, which had the Evolve rock at the front leading the project and the community rocks behind Evolve. I sighed. Took a moment. Asked a few penetrating questions. It was a very animated discussion with the group highly engaged. You should have seen the grin on my face when they presented me with their final result, which was a reverse of the original. The community was leading, with Evolve way at the back there for support when needed. Without this kinaesthetic tool to have the discussion (literally rocks from the car park), I don't know that we would have achieved the same result in such a short time.

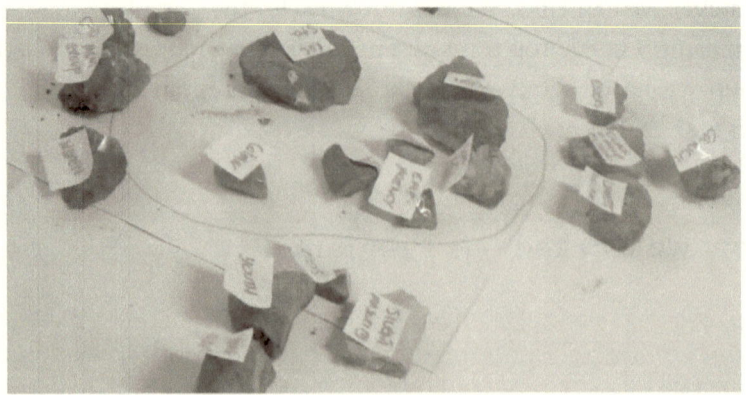

Rocking it in Mt Isa.

How?

We find that the biggest blunders can happen (in lots of situations not just engagement), when people jump to the How or a solution, without thinking through the What, Why and Who first. This can land you in a 'square peg in a round hole' situation. For example, have you ever been in a meeting that feels like it's just not going anywhere, eyes are starting to glaze over, and you are getting frustrated? When in this situation next time, take a step back and ask yourself: have we agreed on the why? Do we have a clear, agreed agenda? Have we worked out what's on the table for discussion? Do we understand the needs of everyone at the meeting (Who)? Chances are that one if not all three of these boxes get a cross.

And when you have done those three things, a meeting might not be the right approach. Some of the items might have been better dealt with offline or one to one, etc.

So, having made your way through the What, Why and Who of our Songlines Pathway, the next step is to match and design your engagement approaches to those.

This is where the real fun begins. There is a rich feast, a smorgasbord of approaches from which to choose. The main thing is to match your approach to the needs of the participants.

We love to mix it up. Everyone varies by cultural background, learning and communication styles (auditory, kinaesthetic, verbal or visual), so we offer different ways to engage. Forget our obsession with the written word. With Aboriginal and Torres Strait Islander Communities for example, we use a lot of visual approaches (like a picture to stimulate discussion and storytelling).

Meeting Marketplace®

Carla

After a decade or more of facilitating community meetings, I noticed that the real stuff would happen in the cuppa conversation. I knew there had to be a better way. So, in the early 2000s, with the help of a Churchill Fellowship, I set off through Australia, New Zealand, Canada and the United States. What I was looking for was a meeting format that could use a range of different approaches to suit the topic and, most importantly, the participants, in a way that would yield a useful and supported outcome. After some experimentation, the 'Meeting Marketplace' emerged: a large group facilitation approach to capture that wealth of information often exchanged during the 'cuppa and yarn'.

After 10 years of running marketplaces, we knew we were onto something and Munya and I worked together to adapt the approach to Aboriginal communities. While a market is not a traditional way of meeting in Aboriginal communities, we kept the name as it captures the essence of what is happening – exchanging and sharing.

So, what does it look like? Just like a market, there are different stalls or activity hubs, with each one offering a different way to participate. There is always an orientation hub, a Café/BBQ and 'group session' to allow for yarning.

Let's share an example from a remote Aboriginal community in North Queensland. The community design team chose the theme of the market and the questions that they would ask, which were around community safety. They ran about five markets in all, each in different locations and at different times. The activities included artwork, storytelling, face painting, and an interactive graffiti wall. We always put on a BBQ and even though we were dealing with tough subjects, there was much laughter and fun.

When we first arrived in the communities, everyone kept saying to Munya and Carla that they wanted a 'town hall meeting'. It was music to our ears when after a short time, people were calling for a 'meeting market' and the markets began popping up somewhat spontaneously.

Munya in action face painting at a Meeting Marketplace

Real-time and Action

This is all about what you do in the moment, when working with people and groups. The most important competency for you to have in undertaking any engagement is cultural awareness and many of these skills have been covered in this book. The great thing is that it is not rocket science. The golden rule still applies – treat people the way you would expect to be treated. Being helpful and friendly is particularly appreciated. Genuine respect for others' beliefs, opinions and lifestyle is essential.

It is crucial to maintain and build the relationship. We have a saying that what you do before a meeting is almost as important as what you do during a meeting, which is almost as important as what you do after. In short, what you do after a meeting can be the most impactful. Get back to people and let them know how your conversations made a difference. Our connection is circular - an on-going feedback loop and relationship. You work out your success criteria at the beginning, and then you stop to reflect, evaluate and adapt.

Our Top Engagement Tip

So, if we only had a minute with you to summarise all the above it would be this. Having some cultural awareness training is important *before* you engage with Aboriginal and Torres Strait Islander communities. In preparation, follow the steps of What, Why, and Who before you get to the How. When you are out there, mix it up (your approaches). Be creative, enjoy, and have fun while making wonderful connections. Follow up and always get back to people about how their involvement made a difference.

All of the above principles apply whether face to face or online. As an example, every activity that we have described in this book which is part of our 7 Step cultural awareness program, is done whether face to face or online. Alot is possible in an online meeting, you just need to make sure that you are applying great engagement and facilitation strategies. We can forget this, and drop the ball so to speak when it comes to online engagement.

CULTURAL PROTOCOLS

In the second part of this chapter, we share some important cultural protocols to be aware of in your engagement work. Cultural protocols are all about showing respect. The following protocols are a guide only and care should be taken not to generalise or stereotype but to find out how they may differ in a particular locality. Here are some key ones to know.

How do I Refer to Indigenous Peoples?

An important way to show respect is to use the right terms when referring to the Indigenous peoples of Australia. Some terms are considered inappropriate and/or offensive because of their racist history. For example, the use of 'full-blood' or 'part' Aboriginal was enshrined in legislation that defined Indigenous identity along racial lines and effectively ignored Indigenous self-identification and expression. Aboriginal and Torres Strait Islander people do not see themselves in terms of blood quantum but as whole human beings. The use of 'people' or 'peoples' immediately after the terms 'Aboriginal' and 'Torres Strait Islander' reinforces this respect.

Ways to Show Respect

- Keep it simple and use plain English always.
- Find out and listen to what names people choose to identify themselves by (e.g. Koori/Koorie), and only use this name if you have checked that this is ok.
- Take care to learn to pronounce words properly, including someone's name and their group identity. When in doubt, always ask. Most people will appreciate your genuine interest and care.

- Terms that are okay to use: Aboriginal and Torres Strait Islander peoples, First Peoples, Indigenous Australians, First Nations, or First Australians. Capitalisation as per these examples reinforces this respect.

Ways that are Considered Disrespectful

- Using inappropriate and/or offensive terms such as 'Aborigine', 'half-caste', 'full-blood', or 'part' Aboriginal.
- Using acronyms when referring to Aboriginal and Torres Strait Islander peoples such as ATSI.
- Using shortened names such as 'Abo' or 'Indig'.
- Saying an Aboriginal person has gone 'walkabout'. This phrase is offensive because it misrepresents Aboriginal culture.

Communicating Respectfully

There are a range of protocols covering the reporting, publication, broadcasting and representation of Aboriginal and Torres Strait Islander people in media and publications. These protocols apply to all communications including social media, print collateral, websites and other multimedia productions.

- Publish a warning at the start of publications as a mark of respect to people who have passed away. For example: Aboriginal and Torres Strait Islander people should be aware that this [DVD/video/program/website, etc.] may contain the voices and images of people who have passed away.
- Seek the permission and consent of local Indigenous communities when photographing or filming on their lands.

- Always seek permission to publish artwork from the artist and acknowledge them.
- Appropriately remunerate Indigenous people for their intellectual property when creating and using artwork.
- Don't use artwork from the internet without seeking permission from the artist.
- Always seek approval from Traditional Owners when erecting Acknowledgment of Country and flags in physical places.

Using Images and Voices

In the Indigenous community, when a person has passed away their names are not mentioned as a mark of respect. People become distressed to see their photographs or hear their voice in radio broadcasts, film and television. In some instances, it may be permissible to name a person who has passed away but only when appropriate permission is obtained from senior living relatives. It has become common practice to insert disclaimers in publications warning people in advance that it may contain the images, voices or names of deceased persons.

Using Indigenous Artwork

There are many cultural protocols governing the reproduction of certain artwork. This is because cultural knowledge is specific to one's age, gender or clan membership. For example, one clan may have the sole right to speak about, tell stories about or draw 'Crocodile Dreaming' or 'Wandjina dreaming'. For this reason, consider when commissioning a local Indigenous artist that their images may be suitable to the local community but may have different cultural meaning and significance in another region. Who can speak on a particular Dreaming or reproduce it in art can be ascertained by seeking advice from Elders in the local community.

Using Affirming Language

When writing about or speaking with Aboriginal and Torres Strait Islander people, it is important to use affirming language. This not only means using the correct terms (see glossary) but avoiding negative, or disparaging descriptions. It is not about being politically correct but about showing respect and being mindful of the way that negative assumptions in language can harm or belittle people. By using affirming language, we can shift intrinsic perspectives about our First Peoples.

Working with Elders and Traditional Owners

Elders are men and women of high degree within the Aboriginal and Torres Strait Islander community who have specialised knowledge, wisdom and a deep understanding of their culture. Being of mature age does not necessarily mean that someone is a recognised Elder and some communities may have very few Elders because of the shorter life expectancy of the Aboriginal and Torres Strait Islander population. Some Elders are referred to as Aunty or Uncle, but you should only refer to these titles when given permission to do so. If in doubt, ask.

Respect for Country

Aboriginal and Torres Strait Islander peoples' relationship to the land is inextricably tied to their cultural and spiritual identity and is usually a specific geographic location which they proudly refer to as their

'Country'. First Peoples have a deep, abiding love for their land that is as profound as their love for family and community.

Caring for Country

Caring for Country activities are based on the traditional laws and customs of Indigenous people that they have inherited from their ancestors and ancestral beings. It is intricately linked to maintaining cultural life, identity, autonomy and health.

As mentioned in Chapter two, there are two distinct cultural protocols when doing business on Country:

- Welcome to Country; and
- Acknowledgement of Country.

Both are important ways of acknowledging and paying respect to Aboriginal and Torres Strait Islander peoples' connection to and continuing relationship with their traditional lands.

Welcome to Country

Aboriginal and Torres Strait Islander peoples have always extended the hand of friendship by welcoming people to their land and providing a safe passage. Only an Aboriginal or Torres Strait Islander person can give a Welcome to Country. It is part of a formal ceremony that takes place at the very beginning of a public event or meeting held on Country. A Welcome to Country may consist of a single speech or include a performance involving dance and music. In some cases, a traditional smoking ceremony may accompany the welcome. This will differ for each community. The Welcome should then be followed by an Acknowledgement of Country.

Acknowledgement of Country

Unlike the Welcome to Country, anyone can make an Acknowledgement to Country regardless of whether they are Indigenous or not. An Acknowledgement of Country takes place as the first address to the audience at a meeting, event or ceremony. It is an acknowledgement of the Aboriginal or Torres Strait Islander community as the traditional owners of the land and the special respect held for their Elders. It also allows non-Indigenous people an opportunity to share and participate in Indigenous culture. This has enormous implications for our journey together on the road to reconciliation and our shared heritage.

How do I say it?

You will hear many ways of acknowledging Country. Evolve takes the view that there is not just one way of doing it. The key to giving an acknowledgement is to know the name of the traditional people on whose land you are on. It is common to acknowledge their Elders, past and present. Some people choose to acknowledge 'emerging' leaders but that is a matter of choice. Don't worry about the correct wording to an Acknowledgement of Country or be too prescriptive. You don't want it to read like an official 'script' at the risk of sounding insincere. It's more important to speak from your heart ensuring the Acknowledgement is authentic, genuine and less formulaic.

Gifts and Payments

In providing cultural services such as Welcome to Country, artistic performances and ceremonies, it is important to acknowledge that Aboriginal and Torres Strait Islander people are using their intellectual property. As such, people should be appropriately remunerated for their services. These fees should cover travel costs for Elders and their support persons as they may require special assistance to get to events. While gifts are a lovely gesture they should never be given in lieu of payment for services. Gift giving plays an important role in Aboriginal and Torres Strait Islander cultures and in some cases, there are complex cultural protocols around this practice. It is best to seek advice from the local community organisation to find out what gifts are suitable.

Smoking Ceremonies

Smoking ceremonies are usually undertaken to cleanse and purify people and spaces before a ceremony takes place. They are also used in traditional healing practices to strengthen the individual and community. An Aboriginal person of high standing and specialised cultural knowledge, usually an Elder, typically performs a smoking ceremony. It may accompany a Welcome to Country but not always. This can be clarified in advance during the planning and negotiation stage.

The authors at a smoking ceremony with Uncle Max Dulumunmun

Flying Flags

There are many things you can do to make your workspace or office a welcoming place for Indigenous people. One way to be inclusive is to display both the Aboriginal and Torres Strait Islander flags in your office to demonstrate your respect for their cultures. Care should be taken to ensure they are correctly displayed. Official government protocol requires that the Australian flag is always flown on the far left, with the Aboriginal flag in the middle and the Torres Strait Islander flag on the right. Where possible, the flagpoles should be at the same height.

Chapter 8 Takeaways

- It is essential to involve Indigenous people in the design of any engagement.

- Having some cultural awareness training is important before you engage with Aboriginal and Torres Strait Islander communities.

- In preparation, follow the steps of What, Why, and Who before you get to the How. When you are out there, mix it up (your approaches). Be creative, enjoy, and have fun while making wonderful connections.

- Follow up and always get back to people about how their involvement made a difference.

- Mutual respect is vital to developing and building partnerships of trust.

- Following cultural protocols and using correct terminology will help in developing trust.

Action:

Prepare yourself for your next project with our complimentary Songlines Pathways® Engagement Checklist, downloadable from practicalreconciliation.com.

Next Steps – What you can do

We have covered a lot of ground in this book and hope that you have enjoyed the journey, and perhaps learnt something about yourself, as well as your Aboriginal and Torres Strait Islander brothers and sisters.

In our introduction, we mentioned that about 1 in every 30 people is Aboriginal or Torres Strait Islander. We also emphasised that to reconcile, one person cannot carry the load of 29 others. If reconciliation is about strengthening relationships between Aboriginal and Torres Strait Islander peoples and non-Indigenous peoples, for the benefit of all Australians, we all have a part to play.

Our vision at Evolve is to create a kinder and more inclusive Australia.

What is your vision? What is your hope? For yourself? For our children and grandchildren? What would you like Australia to look like for them?

We finish our workshops with an invitation for participants to commit to one action. Having undertaken the course and reflected on what they have learnt, we ask them to think of one thing they can do.

This can be as simple as watching a movie like *Rabbit-Proof Fence* or having a go at doing an Acknowledgement of Country.

So, our invitation to you now is to do something. Take action no matter how small. Don't leave it to that one person. We can all do something to create a kinder and more inclusive Australia.

So now it's over to you.

Doorrbajoo

(Good luck in Bardi).

Glossary

Aboriginal: The First Peoples of Australia but excludes those of the Torres Strait region.

Business: The cultural responsibilities and obligations of both men and women. These responsibilities are gendered and referred to as either 'Men's Business' or 'Women's Business' and are separate traditions.

Country: An Aboriginal English term used to describe their traditional lands to which they belong and their place of Dreaming. Aboriginal language usage of the word 'country' is much broader than standard Australian English.

Community: Important elements of a community are country, family ties and shared experience. Community is about interrelatedness and belonging and is central to Aboriginality. Aboriginal and Torres Strait Islander people may belong to more than one community.

Conciliation: The action of mediating between two disputing people or groups.

Corroboree: An Eora word that describes a cultural ceremony involving song and dance. Although other Aboriginal nations have their own distinct terms for 'corroboree', it is commonly used by all Aboriginal groups to refer to these cultural gatherings.

Custodian: A person charged with maintaining and passing on cultural knowledge through art, song and dance, stories, rituals and language.

Deadly: An Aboriginal English word for 'fantastic', 'great' or 'awesome'. It is used in a positive sense as opposed to something negative. This has important implications for Indigenous healthcare and treatment of chronic diseases where a medical practitioner may refer to something as 'deadly' meaning harmful as in diabetes or heart disease. Awareness of this difference in meaning in the Indigenous context is important.

Dreaming/Dreamtime: The Dreaming has different meanings for different Aboriginal groups who each have their own Indigenous terms for their spirituality. The Dreaming is an embodiment of Aboriginal creation which gives meaning to everything. It establishes the rules governing relationships between the people, the land and all things for Aboriginal people. Dreamtime refers to the creative period and is a common term used to describe Aboriginal religion or spirituality. It should always be spelt with a capital 'D'.

Dreaming Beings: Aboriginal Ancestors that created the world that are remembered in story, song and dance. There are many different Dreaming Beings among the nations, the most significant being the Rainbow Snake, the Seven Sisters (Pleiades) and the Two Men (*Wati Kutjara*). These beings traversed the land, sea and sky creating *songlines* and other cultural networks along the way.

Elder: Key person and keeper of knowledge who is highly respected and consulted due to their experience, wisdom, knowledge, background and insight. Being an elder does not necessarily equate with mature age but the degree of cultural knowledge held by an individual regardless of their gender.

Family: Indigenous concepts of family extend beyond narrow biological perceptions of the nuclear family toward more inclusive, complex biological and social ties and structures that embrace an entire community. This wider view of family has a significant impact on kinship obligations and responsibilities.

Gudia: A common term used in the Kimberley to describe a non-Indigenous person. Initially used to describe white people of European origin, it is now extended to all non-Indigenous people.

Homeland: Located on Aboriginal ancestral lands with cultural and spiritual significance to Aboriginal people who live there. Complex connections to land include cultural, environmental and spiritual and obligations, including protection of sacred sites.

Indigenous: Native to a place or area, originating in and characterising a region or country.

Kinship: Includes the importance of all relationships, and of being related to and belonging to the land.

Law Business: Natural Law not western law as in case law or legal precedent. Rather, it refers to the cultural laws of Aboriginal people that was laid down in the Dreamtime by Dreaming Beings. To understand the difference between *law* and *lore*, see Munya's analysis in *Journey Into Dreamtime* at p. 18.

Mob: A colloquial term that many Indigenous people use to identify their people or communities. It is not considered offensive to ask an Indigenous person who their 'mob' is.

Nation: A group of Aboriginal people who share the same language and area of land, river and sea that is their traditional land.

Native Title: A form of land title which recognises Aboriginal and Torres Strait Islander people as rightful owners of that land.

Reconciliation: Defines respecting Aboriginal and Torres Strait Islander peoples by acknowledging them as the First Peoples of Australia. It is about working together as Australians to create a more just and inclusive society. Most First Australians question the true meaning of reconciliation but have generally come to accept its usage.

Respect: Having due regard for someone's feelings, wishes, or rights.

Shared history: Recognises that Australia's history began long before 1788. Since then, Indigenous and non-Indigenous Australians have occupied the same country and shared a destiny that is based on recognising and respecting the rights of all Australians beginning with Aboriginal and Torres Strait Islander peoples as the original inhabitants.

Terra Nullius: A Latin term meaning 'empty land'. It was used as part of legal fiction to justify the colonisation and dispossession of Aboriginal and Torres Strait peoples from their lands.

Traditional Owner: As described in Native Title legislation, an Aboriginal or Torres Strait Islander person or group directly descended from the original inhabitants of a culturally defined area of land or sea. They are the clans, nations and groups who have traditional connections to the land and waters relating to their area that retain decision-making powers in relation to that land or area.

Torres Strait Islander: The First Peoples of the Torres Strait region, as compared to the mainland people.

Glossary

Yarn: An informal conversation or telling a story in a culturally safe environment.

Yarning circle: Culturally safe conversations that take place in a circle.

Bibliography

Munya Andrews *Journey Into Dreamtime*, Ultimate World Publishing, 2019.

Judy Atkinson *Trauma Trails, Recreating Songlines: The Transgenerational Effects of Trauma in Indigenous Australia*, Spinifex Press, 2002.

Milton J. Bennett [ed] *Basic Concepts of Intercultural Communication: Selected Readings*, Intercultural Press, 1998.

Anne Bishop *Becoming an Ally: Breaking the Cycle of Oppression in People*, Zed Books, Second Edition, 1995.

R.M.W Dixon *The Languages of Australia*, Cambridge University Press, 2010.

R.M.W Dixon *Australia's Original Languages*, Allen & Unwin, 2019.

Diana Eades *Aboriginal Ways of Using English*, Aboriginal Studies Press, 2013.

Edward Hall *The Dance of Life: The Other Dimension of Time*, Anchor Books, 1989.

Edward Hall *The Silent Language*, Anchor Books, 1973.

Max Dulumunmun Harrison *My People's Dreaming*, Finch Publishing, Sydney, 2009.

Russell Means & Bayard Johnson *If You've Forgotten the Names of the Clouds, You've Lost Your Way*, CreateSpace Independent Publishing Platform, 2013.

William B. McGregor *The Languages of the Kimberley, Western Australia*, Routledge, 2004.

David Mowaljarlai & Jutta Malnic *Yorro Yorro*, Magabala Books, 1993.

Anna Haebich *For Their Own Good: Aborigines and Government in the South West of Western Australia*, University of Western Australia, 1988.

Bruce Pascoe *Dark Emu* Magabala Books, 2014 & 2018.

Gracie Greene et al *Tjarany Roughtail: The Dreaming of the Roughtail and Other Stories*, Magabala Books, 2006.

Jodi Picoult *Small Great Things*, Ballantine Books, 2016.

Deborah Bird Rose *Nourishing Terrains: Aboriginal views of landscape and wilderness*, Australian Heritage Commission, Canberra, 1996.

Stay Connected

To go deeper, for each step, we have a range of fantastic resources and learning materials. You will find these at practicalreconciliation.com

For regular updates, tips and ideas we would love for you join the Evolve Community at www.evolves.com.au

Special Offer

The Seven Steps to Practical Reconciliation™

From the bottom of our hearts, thank you for reading this book.

It's a privilege for any author. But for us, it's even more special, and that's because you're now equipped to make very real change. This can kickstart a lifelong journey of learning that will **vastly improve life for Aboriginal and Torres Strait Islander people.**

It's a big deal.

So as a token of our gratitude, we are giving you access to an exclusive deal only available to *Practical Reconciliation* readers just like you.

Here's what you'll get:

If you're an individual
For $50, our special package for individuals is designed to give you an advantage both in the workplace, and in life outside work. You'll get **exclusive access to our Seven Steps On-Demand training** - an interactive, entertaining training program that we usually only offer to organisations. You'll also receive **a special webinar on Practical Reconciliation**, with further tips on how you can be an ally.

Simply head to evolves.com.au/7steps and enter your special code IND7STEPS at the checkout to claim your discount.

If you're a leader at your organisation
They say change starts at the top – which is why exciting things are just around the corner.

Because you've read this book, your team can now enjoy a **20% discount on our popular Seven Steps On-Demand program!** You'll experience a more harmonious workplace in less time than it takes to have lunch.

To claim, visit evolves.com.au/7steps and enter your special code ORG7STEPS.

Speaker Bio

Regarded by Melbourne University as a 'leading Australian thinker', Aunty Munya Andrews is an accomplished Indigenous author and barrister with degrees in anthropology and law. Educated in Australia and the USA, Munya is fascinated by comparative religions, languages, mythology and science and intrigued by the way in which they interact and inform each other. Her second book, *Journey into Dreamtime* is an easy guide to Aboriginal spirituality that explains Dreamtime concepts in a simple way. Munya's life purpose is to create better understanding and appreciation of Aboriginal people, leaving behind a legacy of Dreamtime wisdom for generations to come.

When most of her friends were having their gap year in Europe in the late 80s, Carla Rogers set off for the remote Kimberley, inspired by a longstanding desire to learn from our First Nations people. In her journey since, Carla continues to evolve innovative solutions for engagement and facilitation. An adventurous and creative soul, Churchill Fellow, highly respected program designer and facilitator, what is most important to Carla is kindness. Her dream is to create an inclusive Australia that honours and respects our First Nations people and culture.

Aunty Munya and Carla make a pretty remarkable team. It's little wonder that they are highly sought after as professional speakers and facilitators that entertain, enthral and captivate their audiences.

They are not to be missed.

You can book Aunty Munya and Carla to design and deliver a highly interactive, engaging session for your team on any topic related to practical reconciliation and for Munya, Indigenous wisdom.

Visit www.evolves.com.au/bookevent to find out more

Notes

ARTWORK AND ILLUSTRATIONS BY

RHYS PADDICK

@THE_WHOLESOME_YAMATJI

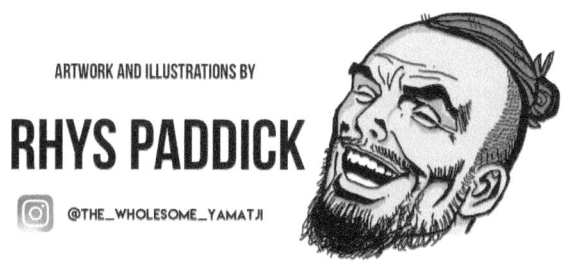

www.ingramcontent.com/pod-product-compliance
Lightning Source LLC
Chambersburg PA
CBHW021148080526
44588CB00008B/259